FLOYD CLYMER'S MOTORCYCLIST'S LIBRARY

The Second Book of the
VESPA

A Practical Handbook covering all 125 and 150 cc models from 1959 to 1963 and 150 cc GS models from 1955 to 1963

John Thorpe

ANNOUNCEMENT

By special arrangement with the original publishers of this book, Sir Isaac Pitman & Son, Ltd., of London, England, we have secured the exclusive publishing rights for this book, as well as all others in THE MOTORCYCLIST'S LIBRARY.

Included in THE MOTORCYCLIST'S LIBRARY are complete instruction manuals covering the care and operation of respective motorcycles and engines; valuable data on speed tuning, and thrilling accounts of motorcycle race events. See listing of available titles elsewhere in this edition.

We consider it a privilege to be able to offer so many fine titles to our customers.

FLOYD CLYMER
Publisher of Books Pertaining to Automobiles and Motorcycles

2125 W. PICO ST.   LOS ANGELES 6, CALIF.

INTRODUCTION

Welcome to the world of digital publishing ~ the book you now hold in your hand, while unchanged from the original edition, was printed using the latest state of the art digital technology. The advent of print-on-demand has forever changed the publishing process, never has information been so accessible and it is our hope that this book serves your informational needs for years to come. If this is your first exposure to digital publishing, we hope that you are pleased with the results. Many more titles of interest to the classic automobile and motorcycle enthusiast, collector and restorer are available via our website at www.VelocePress.com. We hope that you find this title as interesting as we do.

NOTE FROM THE PUBLISHER

The information presented is true and complete to the best of our knowledge. All recommendations are made without any guarantees on the part of the author or the publisher, who also disclaim all liability incurred with the use of this information.

TRADEMARKS

We recognize that some words, model names and designations, for example, mentioned herein are the property of the trademark holder. We use them for identification purposes only. This is not an official publication.

INFORMATION ON THE USE OF THIS PUBLICATION

This manual is an invaluable resource for the classic motorcycle enthusiast and a "must have" for owners interested in performing their own maintenance. However, in today's information age we are constantly subject to changes in common practice, new technology, availability of improved materials and increased awareness of chemical toxicity. As such, it is advised that the user consult with an experienced professional prior to undertaking any procedure described herein. While every care has been taken to ensure correctness of information, it is obviously not possible to guarantee complete freedom from errors or omissions or to accept liability arising from such errors or omissions. Therefore, any individual that uses the information contained within, or elects to perform or participate in do-it-yourself repairs or modifications acknowledges that there is a risk factor involved and that the publisher or its associates cannot be held responsible for personal injury or property damage resulting from the use of the information or the outcome of such procedures.

WARNING!

One final word of advice, this publication is intended to be used as a reference guide, and when in doubt the reader should consult with a qualified technician.

Preface

IN preparing a book on such a machine as the Vespa scooter the author finds himself faced with a number of problems and a number of requirements—some of them mutually contradictory.

Rightly, the Vespa has become one of the most popular of all scooters, not only in Great Britain but also throughout the Continent. It has enjoyed an uninterrupted production run of some sixteen years, using the same basic configuration but with a number of important modifications and in a considerable number of different model types.

Some of these are sports machines of quite high performance, which are ridden by knowledgeable enthusiasts. Some are touring machines and ride-to-work models which may be used by riders who, while no less enthusiastic about their mounts, are not so deeply versed in the mechanics of their machines. Each type of machine and, more important, each type of rider has to be taken into consideration.

Since it is possible to do an enormous amount of damage to a precision-engineered job such as the Vespa if the right methods and the right tools are not employed, I have concentrated mainly upon the basic principles of the machine and upon the simpler routine jobs which will give trouble-free running and efficient operation. However, a whole chapter of stripping instructions has also been included as a guide for the enthusiast who wishes to tackle some of the bigger jobs himself. This is, however, intended *only* as a guide, to be used in conjunction with the maker's own Service Manual for the model concerned. That part of each section in this chapter which deals with the engine removal and initial stripping, down to (but not including) breaking the crankcase joints, can also be used by the average owner who, though not wishing to tackle a major overhaul, may nevertheless wish to save as much as possible of the cost by doing some of the work himself. By removing the engine and stripping it of most of the "top hamper" he can then pass to his Vespa agent only the bare minimum of parts to be dismantled, thereby cutting back on labour costs.

Since little has previously been published on the G.S. range of Vespa scooters, I have included data on these sports models from the original VS 1 of 1955. This had its control cables outside the bars. It was superseded, in 1956, by the VS 2 with internal cables and a half-wave rectifier, and in 1956–57 the VS 3, with full-wave rectifier, was marketed. Only minor modifications distinguished the VS 4 of 1958 and the VDS 3 of 1957 but the VS 5, of 1959, featured a redesigned braking system.

Of the 125 c.c. machines, I have dealt with the 152 L2—the first of the "new look" Vespas with smaller overall dimensions—which appeared

PREFACE

here in the spring of 1959, and the rotary-valve model, but have omitted the Rod Type Vespa, and the Models 9, GL 2, 42 L2 and 92 L2.

So, also, with the 150 c.c. models I have restricted myself to the "new look" period which began with the post-1958 VBA. Models thus excluded are the Continental (1958), the 102 L2 (1957), and the 1957–58 Clubman. A section is, however, devoted to the 5 VBA Sportique range introduced in 1961 and extended for 1963.

In closing, I would like to place on record my thanks to Douglas (Sales & Service) Ltd., of Kingswood, Bristol, for the assistance given me in the preparation of this book, and especially for granting permission for the reproduction of illustrations from Vespa Service Manuals.

JOHN THORPE

Contents

1. WORKING ON VESPAS 1
2. GENERAL PRINCIPLES OF THE VESPA 4
   The carburettor—The ignition system—The transmission—
   The cycle parts
3. TOOLS 20
4. ROUTINE MAINTENANCE 23
   Daily task system—Alternative weekly system
5. FAULT TRACING 27
6. WORK ON VESPA ENGINES 32
   A top overhaul—Complete decarbonizing
7. MAJOR WORK ON ENGINE-TRANSMISSION UNITS . . . 40
   125 c.c. 152 L2 model—125 and 150 c.c. rotary-valve Standard and 150 c.c. Sportique—150 c.c. G.S. Vespa—Later models 150 c.c. G.S. Vespa
8. ELECTRICAL EQUIPMENT 56
9. BRAKES, TYRES AND FORKS 67
10. FUEL SYSTEMS AND CARBURETTORS 74
11. DRIVING AND THE CONTROLS—SIDECAR WORK . . . 78
    Appendix A, Lubrication Charts 84
    Appendix B, Plug Recommendations 87
    Appendix C, Tyre Pressure Chart 88
    Appendix D, Carburettor Data 89
    Index 90

1 Working on Vespas

ODDLY enough, it is the Royal Air Force whom Vespa enthusiasts should thank for the fact that they are riding their machines today. Some extremely accurate bombing of the Piaggio aircraft works at Pontedera, Italy, during the Second World War, had left the factory sadly the worse for wear, and its staff were faced with a number of problems. Not the least of these was the job of moving from one end of the vast factory to the other, since the usable sections were few and far between.

To solve the problem, Piaggio decided to build a tiny runabout, powered by a 98 c.c. two-stroke engine placed alongside the rear wheel. It had a modest amount of bodywork and an open frame, forming a platform on which the rider could put his feet. It had small wheels, and a front shield. It was, in fact, the prototype of the Vespa scooter!

Realizing that the whole of Italy was in much the same state as their own factory, with transport disrupted, the Piaggio management decided to market the factory runabout. A design survey was undertaken, the capacity raised to 125 c.c., and the styling improved. The result was the first production version of the Vespa, which appeared in 1946.

The range with which this book deals are later models, mostly built after the autumn of 1958. They include the latest version of the 125 c.c. machine (earlier versions are dealt with in a companion volume in this series); the rotary-vale 150 c.c. Vespas; and the various 150 c.c. Marks of the sporting four-speed Vespa G.S.

In setting out to work on a Vespa scooter, it must first of all be realized that the scooter is very different from a motor-cycle. The most complicated of motor-cycles is still a relatively easy machine to pull to pieces, and it can often be done with a fairly modest tool kit. This is not the case with the Vespa.

The scooter is a machine designed as one unit (Fig. 1). The engine-transmission unit is designed to fit the Vespa, and the Vespa alone. The front forks are tailored expressly for the machine. It is a unity.

Consequently, there has been no compromise in the mechanical layout. Stripping one of these machines calls for a considerable degree of mechanical knowledge and for a formidable number of special tools. Furthermore, the almost inevitable result of trying to make do without these special tools is to cause considerable damage to the machine.

Before beginning work on a Vespa, therefore, you should study this book thoroughly. All the routine maintenance which can easily be done has been set out, together with a number of hints in this chapter on points which may possibly go wrong. Such work is within the compass of most folk who can use a spanner and a screwdriver.

There is, of course, an art even in that. It is a great mistake, for example, to use too much pressure with a spanner. The length of a spanner is calculated to give the right amount of torque for the size of bolt or nut on which it is used *provided* the pressure applied at the other end is hand pressure only. Using the whole arm to turn a spanner—particularly one of

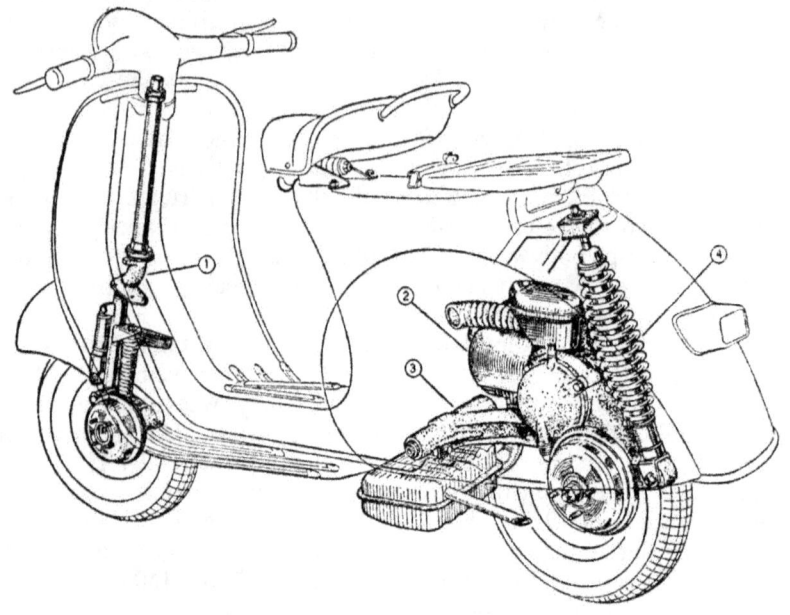

Fig. 1. THE GENERAL LAYOUT OF A TYPICAL VESPA

1. The front fork   3. Rear suspension arm
2. The engine unit   4. Rear spring and damper

the smaller tools, such as a 10-mm open-ender—can result in strained threads or in actual breakage of the bolt or stud.

Of the routine maintenance which you will be performing on your Vespa the most important jobs are those pertaining to the braking system; to the ignition system; and decarbonizing. Keep a careful check on the adjustment of the brakes, for these tend to be deceptive. You will be using them constantly, and each time they are applied they lose a little of their efficiency. This gradual loss of power is so minute, however, that the rider tends to adjust himself, automatically, to the decreasing power of the brakes. Eventually the day comes when they have to be used in an emergency, and to his horror he discovers that they are not half as good as he thought they were. This can be avoided by adopting one of the Task

Systems outlined in Chapter 4. With such a system, a constant watch is kept on not only the brakes but also on all the main units of the machine, so that any incipient fault is noted and rectified before it has had time to develop into one which is serious or potentially dangerous.

So far as the electrical side is concerned, two-strokes are very touchy about their plugs. A faulty plug in a two-stroke engine can imitate any number of horrible mechanical diseases. I have known a faulty plug cause an engine to emit a clanking sound which was a startlingly realistic copy of a smashed big-end. It can simulate petrol starvation, slipped timing, or piston slap. Consequently, always carry a spare plug of known reliability with you, and make a change of plug the first check in any trouble you may encounter.

A whole chapter is devoted to decarbonizing—rightly so, for two-strokes again are dependent upon efficient scavenging if they are to work at all. One word of warning, however: before you start to pull your engine apart make sure that you have somewhere decent to work. Engines should not be stripped when they are dirty, but it is equally wrong to clean an engine and then put the delicate surfaces of the internals on a dirty workbench or a gritty garage floor. Clean newspaper forms an excellent working surface, and parts which have been removed and cleaned can also be wrapped in newspaper and stored away in cardboard boxes until they are ready to be replaced.

In all work on scooters, bear in mind that there are three main requirements: tools, knowledge, and the time in which to do the job. Given these, home maintenance of a scooter can be a pastime almost as enjoyable as riding it.

2 General Principles of the Vespa

ALTHOUGH the Vespa, with its long development history, is both efficient and reliable, to obtain the best from it you must know exactly how it works, and why. This applies not only to the maintenance of the machine, important though that is, but also to its actual use on the road.

So far as engines are concerned, there are two basic types in production for scooters today—the four-stroke engine and the two-stroke. These terms—four-stroke and two-stroke—actually refer to the number of working strokes in one complete cycle of operation of the engine. In the four-stroke engine, then, the working cycle consists of four strokes; in other words, the piston travels from its uppermost position to its lowest, and vice-versa, four times. In an equivalent two-stroke engine it would make only two such trips. All Vespas have two-stroke engines, but to understand this engine it is best to learn how both types operate.

Before considering just how the engine works, it is necessary to know the names of the components. First there is the *cylinder*, which is, as its name implies, simply a metal cylinder. It is closed at one end by a *cylinder head*, which, in the case of a four-stroke, is equipped with *ports* through which gas can flow. For each cylinder there is an *inlet port* and an *exhaust port*. These are closed by *valves*, which are held in the closed position by *valve springs*. To open the valves, a form of mechanical see-saw called a *rocker* is used, one to each valve. It is operated through an arrangement of *push rods* and *cams*.

The lower half of the engine consists of a light alloy case, known as the *crankcase*, on which the cylinder is mounted. Carried on bearings inside the crankcase is the *crankshaft*, usually a pair of heavy flywheels, each with its own half-shaft, joined by a *crankpin*. Though the main shafts are mounted centrally, the crankpin is off-set so that when the crankshaft is revolved the crankpin moves on a circular path. If, then, the crankpin happened to be at the top of the case and the crankshaft was revolved it would not simply rotate, as would the main shafts. Instead it would move at first downward and forward. Once the shaft had been rotated through a right-angle, the pin, while still moving downwards, would begin to move backwards also. After half a turn, it would begin to move upwards and backwards until, in the last quarter-turn, it moved upwards and forwards.

Thus, the end of a *connecting rod* attached to the crankpin would move with the pin in just such a manner. This part of the connecting rod is usually called the *big end*, for the very obvious reason that this particular end of the rod is, invariably, the bigger end.

The other end of the rod, too, has a pin. This is the *gudgeon pin*, and it carries a *piston* made of light alloy. This piston fits closely in the cylinder, in which it is free to slide up and down, but in which it can move in no other way.

If, in this basic engine, the piston is at the top of its travel it is said to be at *top dead centre*, a term usually abbreviated to T.D.C. If it is right at the bottom of its travel it is at *bottom dead centre*, or B.D.C. The distance it must travel between these two points is called the *stroke* and this is normally measured in millimetres.

To understand, first, the four-stroke cycle, imagine that the piston is now at T.D.C. and that the crankshaft is revolving (Fig. 2). As it does so, the

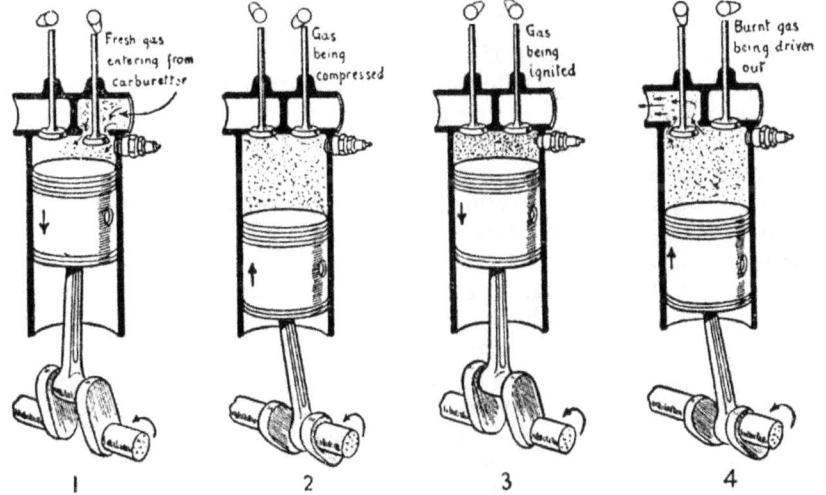

FIG. 2. THE FOUR-STROKE CYCLE

On the four-stroke engine four separate piston strokes constitute a complete cycle. There is no overlapping of strokes as on the two-stroke engine.

crankpin moves, at first, downwards and forwards. This means that the big end of the connecting rod must also move downwards and forwards. Since connecting rods cannot stretch, it exerts a pull on the gudgeon pin, and this, in turn, pulls the piston downwards. The piston, of course, being a tight fit in the bore, is unable to move forwards or backwards. It can only travel up or down. As the piston moves down the cylinder, the valve which has been closing the inlet port is opened. Inside the cylinder, the movement of the piston has lowered the pressure so that it is lower than that of the air outside, and air therefore starts to flow through the inlet port into the cylinder. On its way it is mixed with petrol to form a mixture which can be burned.

This induction of combustible mixture continues for the whole period during which the piston is travelling down the cylinder, and this stroke is consequently called the *induction stroke*.

After half a revolution of the crankshaft, the downward movement of the piston ends, since the crankpin must now begin to press the connecting rod upwards. Obviously, if the inlet port were to be left open, all the mixture which had just been induced would simply be blown out again, and the valve is, therefore, so arranged that it closes at this point. The rising piston now compresses the mixture, and this gives the second stroke of the cycle, the *compression stroke*.

By the time the piston reaches T.D.C. on this stroke, the mixture in the cylinder has been squeezed into the tiny "combustion chamber" formed between the top of the piston—the *crown*—and the inside surface of the cylinder head. On a scooter this chamber will have a volume only about one-seventh that of the cylinder itself. The ratio between this and the *swept volume*—the amount of mixture induced into the engine—is called the *compression ratio*, and this is one of the vital factors in deciding the characteristics of an engine. In the case quoted here the compression ratio would be 7 to 1. If the mixture had been compressed into one-tenth of its original volume it would have been 10 to 1.

Once the gas has been so compressed it is ready to be burned. A spark occurs and ignites the mixture, which burns rapidly. In doing so it expands, so that it can no longer be contained within the tiny combustion chamber. It exerts pressure upon every surface around it, but of these only one can move. This is the piston crown, and the effect of igniting the mixture is to create a pressure inside the combustion chamber which thrusts the piston down the cylinder on the third of its four strokes, the *power stroke*. This time, there is no question of the piston being *pulled* down by the crankpin. On the power stroke it is the piston which thrusts the connecting rod down. And the rod, in turn, causes the crankpin to revolve, thereby turning the flywheels and rotating the main shafts. These drive the vehicle through the medium of gears and chains.

One further stroke remains to complete the cycle, the *exhaust stroke*. When the piston reaches B.D.C. the driving force behind it is largely spent. Now the burnt gases must be cleared out of the cylinder. Carried by the momentum stored in the flywheels, the piston starts to rise. As it does so, the second valve in the cylinder head, the exhaust valve, is opened. The rising piston pushes the burnt gases up the cylinder and out of the exhaust port. At T.D.C. the exhaust valve again closes the port, the inlet valve opens, the piston begins to descend once more, fresh mixture is induced, and another cycle of operations has begun.

That, then, gives us the basic four-stroke cycle: induction, compression, power, exhaust. Induction and power are downward strokes; compression and exhaust upward strokes. With the two-stroke engine all this is rearranged to occur in only two strokes (Fig. 3). The object is to give a smoother-running engine by arranging a power stroke to occur on each downward stroke, whereas the four-stroke only fires on alternate downward strokes. Also the two-stroke is intended to provide an altogether simpler sort of engine. Like the four-stroke it has a crankcase, crankshaft, cylinder, piston and cylinder head, but it has none of the complicated valve gear necessary to make a four-stroke work.

Paradoxically, although it is so much simpler in construction, it is less simple in its manner of operation, since there are always at least two things happening at once. This stems from the fact that the mixture is not, in the first instance, induced straight into the cylinder but, instead, enters the crankcase, which is made specially gas-tight for this purpose. Since there

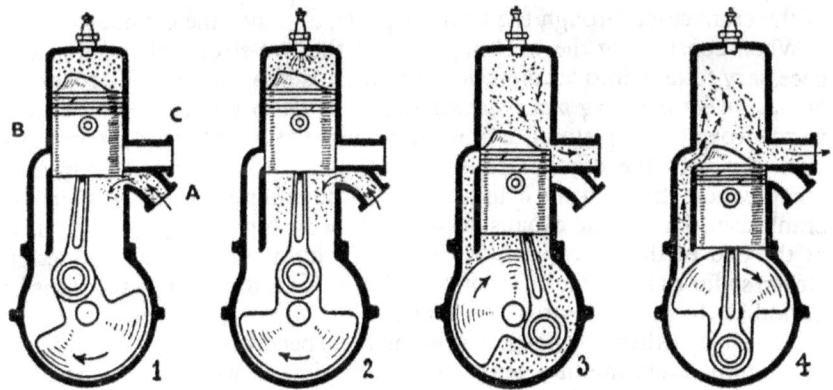

FIG 3. FOUR PHASES IN THE TWO-STROKE CYCLE

Phases 1 and 2 occur during each upward piston stroke, and phases 3 and 4 during each downward stroke.

are no valves, all this mixture is distributed through ports which are covered and uncovered by the movement of the piston, and these are consequently located at the base of the cylinder instead of being placed in the cylinder head.

Imagine a two-stroke engine in which the piston is at B.D.C. after a power stroke. At just this moment the last remnants of the burnt gas will still be streaming out of the exhaust port in the base of the cylinder, and two streams of fresh gas entering through a pair of opposed *transfer ports*. These connect the crankcase with the cylinder and are sometimes placed opposite one another so that, as the two gas streams enter the cylinder, they collide and deflect each other upwards, away from the exhaust port. Vespas, however, have a piston crown specially shaped to do this job, a type known as a *deflector piston*.

The piston now begins to travel up the cylinder. First, its upper edge covers the transfer ports, thus sealing the crankcase. Almost immediately afterwards it closes the exhaust port, and the cylinder, too, is sealed. The rising piston now begins to compress the fresh charge trapped in the cylinder, in exactly the same way as in the four-stroke engine.

As the piston nears T.D.C., its lower edge (*skirt*) uncovers the inlet port and a charge is drawn into the crankcase. At T.D.C. a spark occurs in the combustion chamber and the piston is thrust down the cylinder on a power stroke. As it descends it first covers the inlet port with its skirt, and the underside of the piston then begins to compress the mixture in the crankcase.

Towards the end of the stroke the top edge of the piston uncovers the exhaust port, through which the burnt gases are carried by their own momentum. A split second later the top of the piston uncovers the transfer ports, and the underside of the piston begins to pump the fresh charge out of the crankcase, through the transfer ports, and into the cylinder.

When considering the working cycle of the two-stroke, therefore, it is necessary to take into account not only what is happening in the cylinder, *but also what is taking place simultaneously in the crankcase*. Each downward stroke of the piston is a power stroke in the cylinder and a compression stroke in the crankcase. Each upwards stroke of the piston is a compression stroke in the cylinder and an induction stroke (Fig. 4) in the crankcase. There is no exhaust stroke, this being replaced by a mere phase at the end of the power stroke. The same holds true for the induction stroke so far as the cylinder is concerned, for this is replaced by the transfer period as the piston approaches B.D.C.

Obviously, when an engine is running at a speed which may reach 5,000 revolutions every minute, there is very little time in which to perform the vital job of clearing the burnt gas out of the cylinder and replacing it with fresh gas. When, as in the two-stroke, one attempts to cram all this "breathing" into a few milliseconds at the fag end of a stroke, some degree of efficiency is bound to be lost, and this, in fact, is precisely what happens.

Since the two-stroke has twice as many power impulses in a given time as the four-stroke, it might be thought that it would develop twice the power from a given size of cylinder. In practice, it usually develops slightly less power than the equivalent four-stroke. One of the reasons is that, at the higher engine speeds, there is this drastically restricted time in which the engine can "breathe." Another reason lies in the construction of the engine itself. The exhaust port *has* to be opened first, and it follows that if the port is piston-controlled it must therefore close *last*. Consequently it remains open for a short period when the transfers are closed and the piston is ascending. Inevitably, some of the fresh mixture which has just been induced is expelled through the exhaust port and lost.

One aid to greater efficiency is the rotary-valve induction system used on some Vespa models. This enables a longer induction period to be used, but does not involve complications.

Where the two-stroke really gains is at low speeds, since here it has more time to breathe. Consequently it develops greater usable power than could a four-stroke unit, and this is particularly noticeable on hills. In some cases, as on many of the Vespas, this superiority is so pronounced

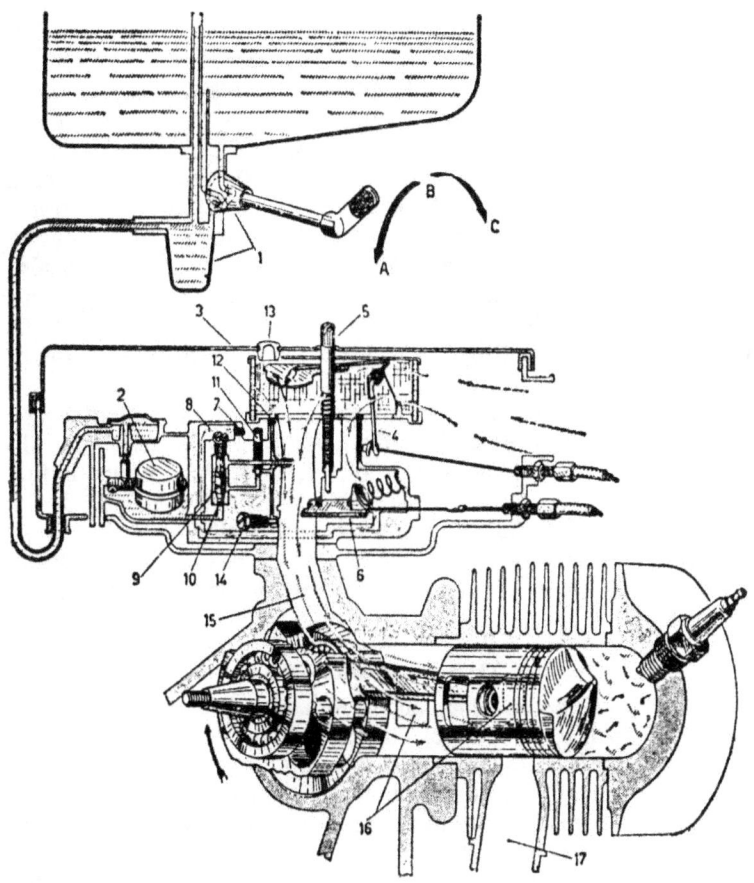

FIG. 4. THE INDUCTION SYSTEM ON A ROTARY-VALVE ENGINE

1. Petrol tap
2. Float
3. Carburettor and air cleaner
4. Choke
5. Throttle stop screw
6. Throttle slide
7. Main jet air vent
8. Air bleed on mixer top
9. Mixer
10. Main jet
11. Idling jet
12. Idling jet air vent
13. Plug for injecting oil when laying up
14. Idling adjuster
15. Induction port
16. Transfer ports
17. Exhaust port

that the two-stroke engine is able to be operated in conjunction with a three-speed gearbox. The more sporting models, of course, have the more complicated four-speed box.

Another great simplification which the layout of the two-stroke engine permits is the use of petroil lubrication. All engines need oil. Not only does it reduce friction, but it also helps to keep the internal surfaces relatively cool.

With a four-stroke, it is necessary to use an independent oiling system, fed by a pump which delivers oil from a sump or oil tank, through passageways to bearings, the cylinder walls, and the valve gear. This is, of course, highly efficient, but it calls for the pump itself, its auxiliary drive, and oil container, filters, drain plugs, and passageways.

The two-stroke, however, has its mixture delivered into the crankcase first. If oil is mixed with this fuel, it means that it can be taken into the case and distributed over the bearings and moving parts without any mechanical complication at all. Furthermore, oily mixture is also fed straight into the cylinder from the crankcase, thus giving continual cylinder-wall oiling—by the incoming mixture on the piston's "cylinder compression" stroke, and by the transfer period at the end of the power stroke.

Crude though it may appear at first glance, the petroil system works well in practice, and it has the added advantage that when climbing hills the engine receives an adequate supply of oil, since the amount induced is proportional to throttle opening and not merely to engine speed. On the other hand, when descending a hill with the throttle closed, the two-stroke can be partially starved of oil, although enough has usually condensed on the crankcase walls to form an inbuilt reserve which offsets this slight disadvantage.

THE CARBURETTOR

We noted, in passing, that when air is induced into the cylinder it is mixed with fuel to form a combustible mixture. This, of course, is a drastic understatement of the magnitude of the job performed by a simple, but precision-engineered, instrument known as the carburettor.

In principle, this is little more than a glorified scent spray with a Gallic name, but it has to carry out one of the most crucial of all jobs—metering out a precise and minute ration of fuel and mixing it thoroughly with air in just the right proportion to enable it to be burned efficiently.

At first sight, this may not appear to be over-exacting, since the ideal ratio is around 1 part of fuel to 14 parts of air. This, however, is the proportion by *weight*; the carburettor operates by *volume,* and on this basis each 100 c.c. of combustible mixture needs to contain only about 0·2 c.c. of fuel, the remaining 99·8 c.c. being air! Obviously the carburettor, despite its simplicity, is a precision instrument and has to be treated accordingly.

The basic components of a carburettor are: a fuel reservoir, called a *float chamber*; a *venturi*, or *choke*, through which air is drawn; jets, which meter the fuel; and a *throttle*, which controls the amount of mixture which can pass through the carburettor and into the engine.

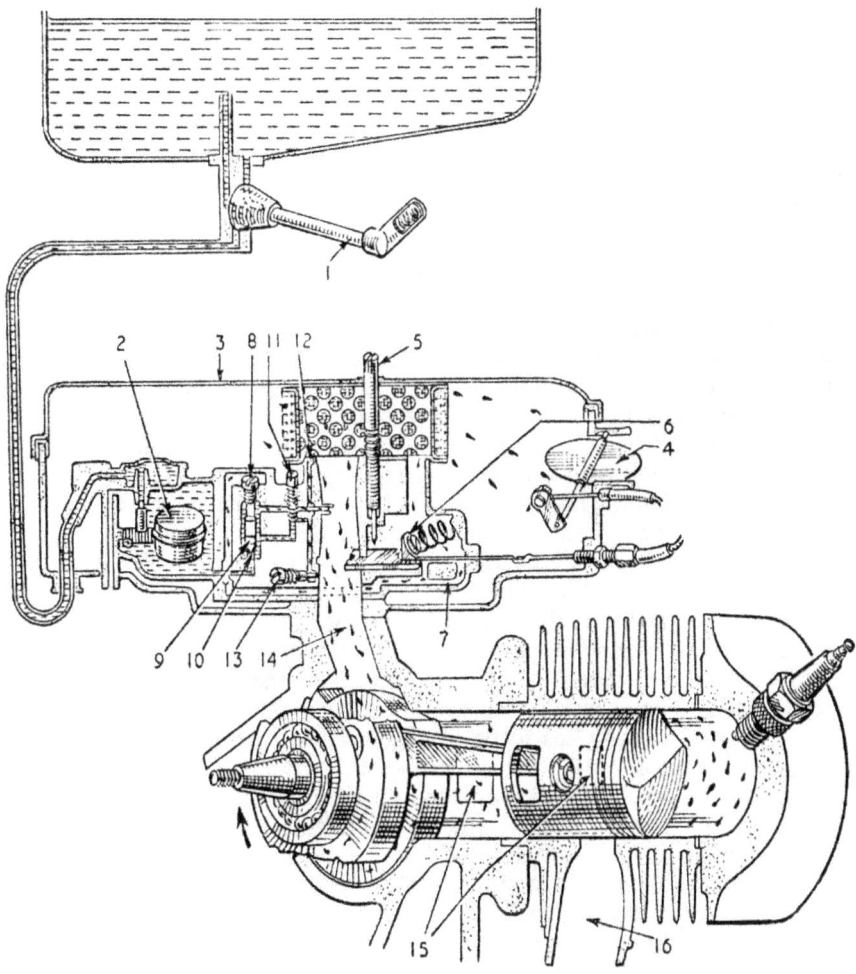

Fig. 5. The Rotary-valve Induction System Used on the 150 c.c. Standard and Sportique Models

1. Fuel tap
2. Float
3. Air cleaner and carburettor
4. Choke
5. Throttle stop screw
6. Throttle slide
7. Main jet air vent
8. Mixer top air bleed
9. Mixer
10. Main jet
11. Idling jet
12. Idling jet air bleed
13. Idling adjuster
14. Induction port
15. Transfer ports
16. Exhaust port

Consider first the basic method of operation (Figs. 4 and 5). Fuel is fed to the float chamber. This is very much like a pocket edition of the familiar domestic cistern. The chamber contains a float, which rises as fuel is admitted through a valve. In rising, the float carries with it a tapered needle, and this needle is carefully contoured to fit in a seat in the valve. When the level inside the chamber is correct, the needle is pressed fully home on its seating, thus cutting off the flow of fuel. When the level in the chamber falls the float falls with it, and so does the needle. Leaving its seating, it thus permits more fuel to flow into the chamber, until the correct level is again reached.

Connecting the float chamber with the body of the carburettor is a drilled passageway through which petrol flows into a *jet well*. A tube is placed vertically in this well so that its lower end is immersed, while the upper end opens into the venturi. Screwed to the bottom of this tube is a *jet*, an essential part of the carburettor which looks suspiciously like a small screw or bolt with a hole drilled through the centre. That, in fact, is just what it is, but the hole is so proportioned that it will pass just the right amount of fuel and no more. When the crankcase induction stroke begins, air is drawn through the carburettor venturi, which is so shaped that there is a fall in pressure in the section—called the *mixing chamber*—around the jet tube. As a result, fuel is drawn up the tube into the chamber, where it mixes with the air, and passes through the inlet port into the crankcase.

Obviously, a carburettor which consisted of these parts alone would work, but the engine would run at only one speed. Some means of varying the supply of mixture has to be arranged, and this means has to be one which keeps the essential fuel-air proportion at all openings.

On earlier Vespas, the solution adopted was to use a *needle jet* to control the fuel flow into the mixing chamber, and to couple this to a *throttle slide* to vary the amount of air admitted. This is how such a system works.

The jet tube is carefully tapered internally to match a long, tapered needle, arranged to move inside it. At the top, this needle is clipped to the air slide, which is itself capable of moving up and down in the carburettor. A cable, connected to the throttle control, pulls it upwards, and a light spring helps to return it when the control is slackened.

At the front of the slide a half-moon shaped area is cut away, and it is this *cut-away* which governs the characteristics of the slide and decides how much air can pass through it at intermediate throttle openings.

When the throttle is closed, only a very small amount of air can pass— so small, in fact, that it is impossible for the main jet to meter out the tiny amount of fuel required. For running under these conditions a very fine jet, called the *pilot jet*, delivers a minute ration of fuel to the mixing chamber, and in the main jet itself the throttle needle is hard against its seating, and no fuel at all passes through.

As the throttle is opened, the slide is raised, and so is the needle. More air passes through the venturi, and the movement of the tapered needle has opened up a passage for fuel through the main jet. Further movement of the throttle increases both the amount of air permitted to pass and the amount of fuel which the jet supplies, until at full throttle both passages are supplying the maximum amounts of which they are capable.

Later carburettors retain the slide, but use internal metering jets in place of the needle and jet tube.

Since the proper action of the carburettor depends upon the operation of very fine metering devices, great attention must be paid to ensuring that the internals are kept free from dirt. Even a speck of dirt is quite enough to block the jet and thus prevent fuel passing through it. The petroil is, therefore, normally filtered at several points by passing through fine wire mesh. One such filter is usually fitted round the inlet of the on/off tap, in the fuel tank, and a second filter protects the needle valve.

When an engine is cold it needs a somewhat richer mixture than usual to enable it to start, and to supply this it is usual to employ a *strangler*, sometimes called, rather misleadingly, a *choke*. This should not, of course be confused with the venturi.

The purpose of a strangler is to cut down the air supply independently of the fuel supply, thus giving the same amount of fuel but mixing it with a smaller supply of air, and a rich-mixture device of this type is invariably some form of plate which is used to block the carburettor inlet. It can be a supplementary slide, a plate which swings over the mouth of the carburettor, or even a form of shutter on the carburettor air filter. Most carburettors, besides being equipped with fuel filters, also have a filter for the air. This is not so much to protect the carburettor as to protect the engine, since the air usually contains dust; and dust, harmless though it may look, contains a surprising number of very hard particles which are quite capable of scratching the working parts of the engine very badly indeed.

An air filter itself forms an obstacle to the air flow and cuts the amount of air entering the carburettor. In the design stage, this obstruction is taken into consideration, and the fuel is metered accordingly. If, therefore, an instrument which is intended to have an air filter is used without one, the effect is to weaken the resulting mixture, since more air is entering while the fuel supply remains unaltered. Damage to the internal parts of the engine apart, this is one reason why the engine should not be run with the air filter removed.

THE IGNITION SYSTEM

Even really experienced riders often have only the slightest knowledge of the working of the electrical system upon which the whole operation of the engine depends. As a result, the electrics are frequently neglected, failure results, and the immediate conclusion is that electricity is thoroughly unreliable anyway! There is no need, however, to be a qualified electrical engineer to understand *how* the system works.

All electrical practice is founded upon circuits, and upon the fact that an electric current will invariably take the shortest path to earth. In this connexion, though, it should be emphasized that "earth" does not necessarily mean the ground. So far as a scooter's electrical system is concerned, "earth" is the mass of the scooter itself, a little world which is all its own.

A circuit is just what its name implies. In this, electricity is rather like a model railway. If all the points are correctly set, the train will go round and round. If they are not so set, it will simply end up standing still.

As with the train, so with electricity. Provided there is a circuit, the current will flow. If the circuit is broken, it will not. And just occasionally there may be some points badly set which direct it straight to earth—a short-circuit—just as if the train had been directed on to a branch line leading straight to the edge of a cliff!

Electricity is measured in *volts* and *amperes*. The *volt* is a measure of its force: the *ampere* basically a measure of the number of electrons per second passing a given point within the electrical circuit. In other words, while voltage indicates the electrical pressure in the circuit, amperes indicate the *quantity* of electricity which is flowing. The resistance to the flow presented by the wires and so forth which make up the circuit is measured in *ohms*, one ohm being a resistance which calls for one volt to be applied so that one ampere may flow.

Electricity is further regarded as comprising two basic types of current—positive and negative—but for all practical purposes it is only necessary to know that these do, in fact, exist.

Finally it is necessary to accept one further basic fact: that when a *coil* is placed in a magnetic field electricity is produced.

Two types of machine for producing electricity are used on engines, the a.c. generator and the d.c. generator. The first produces a form of current which *alternates*, producing a constantly reversing flow. The second produces direct current, which flows in one direction only. On Vespas a d.c. flywheel magneto-generator is employed.

In this design (Fig. 6), permanent magnets are mounted inside the rim of the external flywheel, and a stator plate, bolted to the engine, holds an ignition coil and lighting coils, each being closely-wound coils of fine wire. They are different, however, in that the ignition coil is really two coils in one—a low-tension primary winding surrounding a high-tension secondary winding, but fully insulated from it. Sometimes this coil is mounted externally and current is fed from coils on the stator plate.

There is one other essential part: the contact-breaker. This is simply a mechanical switch, consisting of a pair of points which are opened and closed by a cam carried on the engine mainshaft. Electrically, the contact-breaker is connected into the low-tension side of the ignition circuit.

From the high-tension winding of the ignition coil, a heavily insulated *high-tension lead* is connected to a *sparking plug* set in the cylinder head. This plug consists of a *body*, which screws into the head, and an insulated central *electrode* to which the high-tension lead is connected. Welded to the body is a *side electrode*—some plugs may have several—which is set so that a gap of around 20 thousandths of an inch exists between its tip and that of the central electrode.

When the flywheel is revolved, the magnets set up a magnetic field, and low-tension electricity is generated in the primary windings of the ignition

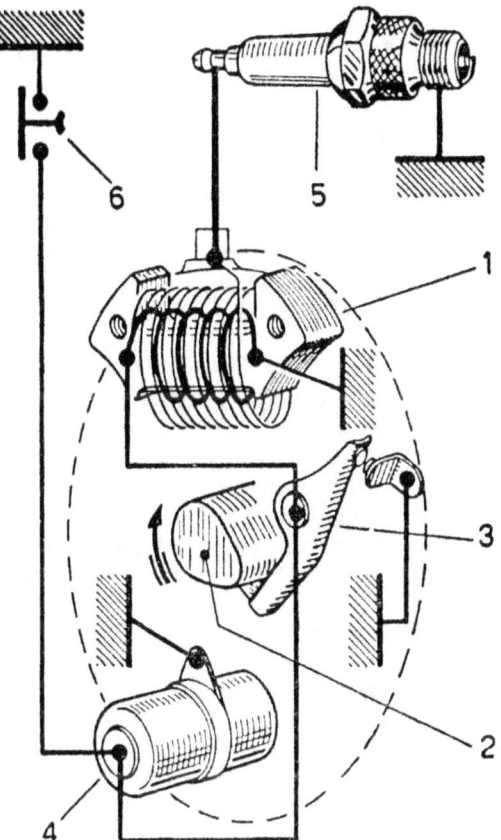

FIG. 6. THE LAYOUT OF A TYPICAL IGNITION SYSTEM

The ignition coil (1) is carried inside the flywheel. A cam (2) works the contact-breaker (3), arcing at the points being prevented by the condenser (4). Current is supplied to the sparking plug (5) and the cut-out switch (6) allows the system to be earthed to stop the engine.

coil. At a predetermined point, however, the cam presses one of the points of the contact-breaker away from the other, and thus breaks the circuit.

Here something happens which has to be taken on trust. This sudden rupturing of the low-tension circuit in the primary windings of the ignition coil creates a high-tension current in the coil's secondary windings. This current is of very high voltage—about 33,000 volts, which is the same as that carried in the conductors of the rural electricity grid system. Seeking the shortest path to earth, this current streaks down the high-tension lead. Normally it would stop dead at the gap in the sparking plug, but the pressure behind it is too great to permit it to do so. Instead, it jumps across the gap in the form of a hot, blue spark, and it is this spark which ignites the mixture in the cylinder. In a normal scooter two-stroke engine this operation can occur some 5,000 times every minute.

To prevent the low-tension current from doing at the contact-breaker points just what the high-tension current subsequently does at the sparking-plug gap—jumping across in the form of a spark—a small electrical "shock absorber" called a condenser is added to the circuit.

The lighting systems and horn can be supplied with electricity from a battery, which is charged by current delivered from the L.T. coils, or this current can be taken direct to the components concerned, which will then operate only when the engine is running.

THE TRANSMISSION

Internal-combustion motors are high-speed engines in which power output is, within limits, proportional to the speed of rotation of the engine. At low speeds, therefore, less power is developed than at high speeds. Where outside factors, such as a hill, increase the load on an engine, its speed, and consequently its power, falls off. This, in turn, reduces its speed still further, causing a further drop in power. At length, the load becomes so great that it overcomes the remaining power of the engine and the motor "stalls."

Basically, there is a comparatively narrow range of engine speed at which the greatest power is developed, and the engine should, ideally, run at this speed whenever possible. The designer does in fact try to arrange for this to coincide with the top-gear cruising speed. To deal with varying loads, however, some means of keeping engine speed high when road speed falls is necessary, and this need is met by the gearbox.

This consists basically of an input and output shaft, on which are carried a series of meshing gears. Each pair of gears gives a different reduction between the speeds of the two shafts. Only one pair of gears can be used to transmit the power at any one time.

Initially, the primary drive, which transmits the crankshaft movement to the gearbox, provides the first reduction in speed, cutting the rotational speed by approximately one half. This is reduced still further in the gearbox itself, depending upon which pair of gears is locked into position on the shafts. In top gear, therefore, the engine crankshaft may revolve 4 times for each revolution of the rear wheel, but in bottom gear it will turn over 12 times. In one revolution of the rear wheel, then, top gear allows the power of 4 power strokes to be applied, but in bottom gear, in the same distance covered, the power of 12 strokes is passed through to the driving wheel. Thus, an increase in load can be counterbalanced by changing into a lower gear, bringing more power to bear in a given distance, at the cost of a drop in road speed.

The method employed to lock the various gears to the shafts is supremely simple. On the input shaft all gears revolve with the shaft; on the output shaft the gears run free, but are constantly meshed with the input gears. Each free-running gear in turn can be locked to the shaft when a sliding member is moved sideways by a *selector*, whose movement is dictated by a twist grip and cable control.

A vital part of the transmission is the *clutch*, which enables the drive to be freed at will. A clutch consists of one member driven by the engine, a second member which is connected to the transmission, and friction plates which link the two, together with springs and a withdrawal mechanism. There is thus no direct connexion between the engine and the transmission. All the drive is taken through the clutch plates. The clutch has two main parts: the clutch centre and the clutch body.

The clutch centre has a series of splines on its boss, and the clutch body a series of splines round its inner periphery. Inside, a pressure plate and a series of clutch plates are fitted. Half these carry friction linings. Alternate plates are splined round the outer edge to match the splining of the clutch body. Strong springs, held by a spring plate, press all these plates hard together. When the clutch is driven by the crankshaft it turns and, owing to the pressure exerted by the springs, the friction between the plates is such that they also turn as one unit and in so doing transmit the drive.

When the withdrawal mechanism is operated the pressure of the springs is relieved. The part of the clutch driven from the engine—and the plates fixed to it—still revolve, but the friction between these and the remaining plates is now too low to transmit movement. The lined plates therefore remain stationary, and so does that part of the clutch fixed to the primary drive. Thus no drive is transmitted.

By gradually releasing the withdrawal mechanism, the revolving plates can be brought into gradual contact with the stationary plates. At first, these "slip," but as contact is increased they speed up, until with the full spring pressure restored the whole clutch is once again rotating as a complete unit. This is what happens each time a scooter moves off from a standstill.

THE CYCLE PARTS

When a scooter is driven along a road it remains upright for exactly the same reason that a gyroscope refuses to topple over; the two revolving wheels do in effect, act as a pair of gyroscopes, and resist all attempts to force them out of their course.

There are, however, other factors which enter into it. One is the design of the steering gear. This is so arranged that, although the fact is not immediately apparent, the front wheel is trailing, rather like the castor of an armchair. The characteristics of the steering depend to some extent upon the amount of *trail* specified by the designer, and to some extent upon other factors. One of these is the *rake*—the angle at which the steering head is set—and others are the weight distribution of the machine as a whole and the position of its centre of gravity.

In addition, the manner in which the suspension systems act plays a great part in determining whether the scooter handles well or not. The Vespa design utilizes a trailing link front fork, in which a short arm carrying the wheel moves upwards and backwards against the resistance of a spring. This movement has to be damped. If there were no damper, the spring would thrust the wheel up and down with a rapid action, and so cause the front end of the machine to pitch up and down.

To prevent this, a hydraulic damper is used. This consists of an oil chamber and a disc valve, so designed that when the sliding member rises it permits the oil to pass through with little or no resistance. On the return stroke the valve is partially closed, and this slows down the rate at which the oil can return to the chamber. In consequence, the return stroke of the trailing link is also slowed down, thereby preventing spring oscillation. A similar layout is adopted at the rear, where the suspension is controlled by a large, coil spring and an independent hydraulic damper.

Just as important as making the scooter move is the ability to make it stop. This is the job of the brakes, which are of internal-expanding type. Each wheel carries a *drum*, the inside surfaces of which are accurately ground so that the drum is completely round and true.

Closing the drum is a *back-plate*, and affixed to this plate is a *pivot pin*. Diametrically opposed to the pin is a cam, which is connected to the brake lever. Two *brake-shoes*—semicircular in shape, with a friction lining riveted to the outer curve on each shoe—are fitted with one end butting on the pivot pin and the other on one face of the cam. They are held together by a spring and the whole back-plate assembly is fixed rigidly to the machine.

When the brake lever or pedal is operated, the cam turns and presses the free ends of the shoes outwards. This brings the friction linings into contact with the inside surface of the drum, decelerating the machine.

A brake is basically a form of heat exchanger. The friction created by the linings rubbing on the surface of the drum absorbs energy which would otherwise be devoted to driving the scooter, and this energy is converted into heat, which is dissipated from the surface of the drum.

Both brakes on Vespas are controlled by cables. In addition, cables are used for the throttle, clutch and gear controls. For efficient operation, a cable depends upon the correct relationship between its inner and outer wires being maintained. Since the inner wires have a tendency to stretch, the outer casings are provided with screwed adjusters which, in effect, enable the effective length of the outer casing to be varied in relation to the inner wire. All cables work either against the resistance of a spring, by which the return action is supplied, or against the pull of a second cable operating in an opposite direction, since cables normally perform well only when used in tension.

3 Tools

It is virtually impossible to make a bigger mistake, when setting out to maintain or overhaul a scooter, than to attempt to do the job with inadequate tools. To carry out even routine maintenance jobs properly calls for the use of a good-quality tool kit, while major overhauls can quite often require the use of special tools. This is certainly the case with the Vespa, since stripping demands the use of tools designed by the manufacturer to do one specific job, and one job only.

Each Vespa is equipped with a tool kit upon delivery, but this is designed to cope only with roadside emergencies and to carry out the major routine jobs. It is not intended for the sterner work of stripping the engine.

The use of special service tools for such jobs as splitting the crankcases is not dictated by cantankerousness on the part of the manufacturer. Nor does it indicate a desire to make a little on the side by selling such tools at an extra profit. It merely reflects the fact that these scooters are precision-engineered. To obtain the performance and reliability of the Vespa the specified tolerances are very close; so close, in fact, that only special tools have the slightest hope of freeing the various components concerned.

Even where the jobs to be tackled do not call for the use of special tools they will still require the use of good tools. Cheap spanners and so forth are a bad investment. They do not wear well, and they also have an infuriating habit of ruining nuts and bolts. Thus, the first essential is to buy a really good set of chrome-vanadium open-ended spanners in metric sizes. A set of half a dozen spanners will give a range of sizes sufficient for most of the work, and will cost only a couple of pounds.

Next, it is vital to have a set of strong metric box-spanners, or, better still, deep-socket spanners. Ring spanners are more of a luxury. They are less handy in confined spaces than are open-enders or sockets, although they do give a very good grip. In addition, you will need a pair of really good screwdrivers, with insulated handles. One screwdriver with a $\frac{5}{16}$-in. blade and an electrical screwdriver with a long $\frac{1}{8}$-in. blade are the minimum requirements. And don't forget your pliers; they are indispensable for electrical work and for use on the control cables.

USING THE TOOLS

There is far more to using even the simplest of hand tools than merely placing them in position and tugging hard. Each particular type of spanner has its own characteristics, and each is better suited for one particular type of job. As you will see from the illustrations in later chapters, which are taken from the official Vespa Service Manuals, the factory places great stress on using the right tools for the job, noting on the drawings not only the spanner size, but also the type that is to be employed.

Open-ended spanners are the great all-rounders of the kit. They can be used in confined spaces and they have the advantage that the jaws are angled, so that reversing the spanner will give fresh purchase on the nut. This is most useful when the nut in question is inaccessible, since it can be freed in stages simply by constantly reversing the spanner.

It is, of course, essential that only the right size of spanner should be used. The open-ender applies its pressure on the flats of the nut or bolt, and is consequently made with jaws of just the right width to grip them. If too large a spanner is used, the jaws will press against the angles of the bolt instead of the flats. One of two things then happens: either the spanner gouges away the metal of the head, leaving a rounded surface which no spanner on earth could ever again grip, or else the bolt head slightly springs the jaws of the spanner itself, which is promptly ruined. Or, of course, you can get the worst of both worlds and ruin both bolt and spanner together!

Damage to the jaws can also be caused by applying excessive force when trying to free a bolt which refuses to budge. There is a temptation, under these circumstances, to slip a piece of piping over the free end of the spanner to increase the leverage. This is permissible provided due care is used, but if you are none too experienced as a mechanic it is inadvisable to try it. You are more likely to spring the spanner's jaws. Use a socket spanner instead, and you will be surprised at the result.

Socket, box- or ring spanners are at a great advantage when it comes to shifting recalcitrant nuts. Rings and sockets both grip on the angles, not the flats, of the bolt and consequently apply pressure at half a dozen points where the open-ended spanner can do so only on two surfaces. A box-spanner can apply its force on both angles and flats, provided it fits well (cheap box-spanners rarely do) but frequently the weak point here is the tommy-bar used to turn the box, which simply bends under the strain. Another drawback with box-spanners is that, owing to the offset between the part of the spanner which holds the nut and the holes through which the tommy-bar passes, the spanner may tend to ride off the hexagon when pressure is applied.

When using a spanner to tighten nuts or bolts it is important to remember that too much force should not be used. Spanners are made long enough to ensure that mere hand pressure applied through the full leverage of the spanner is sufficient to lock the size of nut or bolt for which the spanner is intended. If excessive force is used, the actual material of the bolt can be weakened sufficiently to cause a fracture. This point, too, should be borne in mind particularly when tightening bolts which are threaded into light alloy. Here, the steel bolt is much harder than the material forming the internal threads, and over-enthusiasm with the spanner can easily strip the threads in the hole. The only real solution, then, is to drill out the hole and re-tap it to take a larger-sized bolt.

Pliers, of course, should never be used as a makeshift spanner, since the jaws can never be parallel and the serrated pipe grip is almost perilously liable to slip. A rounded hexagon is the inevitable result if it does.

Adjustable spanners should never be allowed near the machine. They are a butcher's tool, not a mechanic's. True, an "adjustable" can be useful in an emergency, but for workshop maintenance it is best forgotten since, again, the jaws can never be aligned accurately enough to obviate the danger of slipping.

Screwdrivers should have their blades properly ground so that, in side view, the blade is at first concave, and then runs parallel all the way to the tip. This enables it to be seated properly in the slot and to apply its pressure evenly. A screwdriver whose blade is wedge-shaped when viewed from the side cannot seat properly and exerts all its force on the edges of the slot. Understandably, these crumble under the strain, and the screw is useless thereafter.

After use, all tools should be wiped clean, kept in a dry place, and protected from dust by being wrapped in rag. If they are used fairly infrequently they should also be very lightly oiled. The film of lubricant should, of course, be wiped off before they are again used.

4 Routine Maintenance

THERE is, obviously, a difference between routine maintenance—the day-to-day adjustments and minor repairs which all vehicles need—and major overhauls, but both have their place in keeping a scooter in good working order. A scooter repays constant and sympathetic attention to its everyday condition, but certainly does not take kindly to constant stripping of the

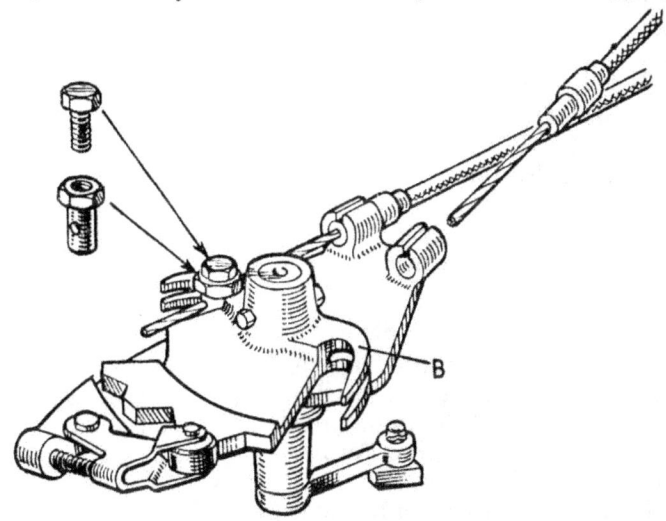

FIG. 7. THE GEAR ADJUSTER ON A VESPA

The cable ferrules operate in the claws (B), adjustment being effected by unlocking the ferrules and varying their positions on the cables.

engine. Oddly, many owners fall into the error of neglecting to give their machines minor attention, while over-conscientiously pulling them apart two or three times each year.

This is the exact opposite of the correct approach. Well driven, and properly maintained, a Vespa will cover 3,500 miles before a top overhaul (a couple of hours' job) is recommended. Some riders have covered well over 10,000 miles without decarbonizing, but the manufacturers frown on such mileages before the engine is attended to. The machine *can* do it; but should not be asked to.

If the routine maintenance is neglected, however, the time which can elapse between overhauls is drastically shortened and the amount of work needing to be done (and the amount of money which needs to be spent) will be much increased.

The reason for this is simple enough. Maladjustments have a cumulative effect. Little enough harm, for example, will result if a sparking plug is loose and the scooter covers 20 miles or so before the fault is discovered. But if, in the absence of a routine check, the loose plug is left for a thousand miles, the results can be serious. All sorts of troubles could spring from this one minor example of neglect. Hot gases could burn away the lower threads in the plug hole, and the wobbling plug could elongate the hole itself. Since the compression would be reduced the engine could never develop its full power, so the performance would fall and the fuel consumption would rise. Extra air drawn in through the plug hole would give a weak mixture, so causing overheating and possible distortion of the barrel and piston. Seizure might result. At the very least, a new head might be required. At worst, you might find yourself paying for a new head, barrel and piston. A pretty stiff price, that, for the minute saved by omitting to make a single, simple check.

Or consider the case of the brakes, which gradually deteriorate in their performance. Unless their power and adjustment is constantly checked you may easily find that when an emergency stop has to be made in a distance of forty feet the scooter will not stop in less than forty-five. The result can be very expensive indeed. It is a dangerously unnecessary way of learning a lesson.

TASK SYSTEMS

Constant and methodical inspection is the best way of preventing troubles, but the usual recommendations, based on elapsed mileage, are difficult to carry out if a full log of the work already done is not kept. This was a problem which faced the Armed Forces some years ago, and to combat it the military authorities evolved Task Systems, which called for a daily or weekly check on each aspect of the mechanical side of a vehicle.

In a modified form such systems are ideally suited for a privately-owned and maintained scooter. They can be of two types, daily or weekly. Which is used depends entirely on the use to which the scooter is put. It if is a "ride to work" machine checks should be made each day. If it is employed solely for week-end excursions a weekly basis can be substituted.

Taking the daily system first, here is a task system for Vespas. It is designed to cover all the major parts which need to be checked, but to carry out these recommendations should never involve the expenditure of more than ten minutes in a single day. In most cases, in fact, only a couple of minutes will be needed.

DAILY TASK SYSTEMS

Sunday. Check the adjustment of front and rear brakes. Check freedom of action of brake controls. Check security of nuts and bolts in braking system. Check lubrication of brake cables.

ROUTINE MAINTENANCE

Monday. Check gearbox oil level. Check all controls for free movement and adequate lubrication.

Tuesday. Check all exposed electrical wiring for signs of abrasion or fracture. Check all electrical terminals for tightness. Check operation of horn, lamps and dip-switch. Check contact-breaker setting.

Wednesday. Examine tyre treads and remove any trapped stones. Check tyre pressures. Check wheels for security. Rock wheels and front fork to check play in bearings.

Thursday. Check clutch cable for adjustment. Check that clutch plates are freeing.

Friday. Check all nuts and bolts for security. Check petroil flow.

Saturday. Check sparking plug for gap and condition. Check battery.

ALTERNATIVE WEEKLY SYSTEMS

Week One. Check gearbox oil level. Check plug for gap and condition.

Week Two. Check brakes for adjustment, freedom and control action,

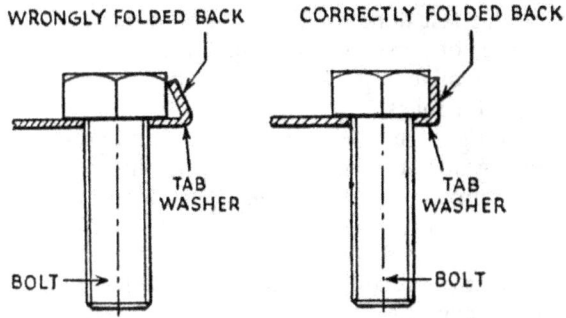

Fig. 8. The Right and Wrong Ways of Folding Back a Tab Washer

These particular parts are on the kickstarter, but the principle holds good for washers on any part of the machine.

and lubrication of cables. Check wheels for security. Rock wheels and front fork to check play in bearings. Examine tyre treads and adjust pressures.

Week Three. Examine all electrical leads for signs of abrasion or fracture. Check all terminals for security. Check operation of horn, lamps and dip-switch. Check contact-breaker setting.

Week Four. Check clutch cable for adjustment. Check that clutch plates are freeing. Check all nuts and bolts for security. Check battery.

By employing this approach to routine maintenance of the Vespa, the rider ensures that most of the major points are checked by the daily system at least once each week. Even allowing for a pretty substantial mileage each day this should mean, at the worst, that no fault could go undetected for more than, say 300 miles. In practice, most defects would be discovered well before they had time to develop to serious proportions.

With the weekly system, a month could elapse between the beginning of a fault and its discovery. Where the machine is used only for a 50-mile week-end jaunt this would be neither here nor there, and so the weekly system would be adequate. If the utilization of the machine is more intense than this, however, settle for daily checks instead.

It is important to remember that the idea is to *check* the relevant points. In nine cases out of ten no adjustment will be necessary: you are only examining the component to find out if it needs to be touched. There is no point in adjusting for its own sake, and where everything is in order you merely leave well alone and pass on to the next point on the list.

Neither system takes into account periodic oil changing and greasing, which still must be carried out on the elapsed mileage basis recommended by the manufacturers. It is all too easy to forget just when the job was last done, and a useful aid to memory in this department is to stick to the parts concerned a piece of self-adhesive tape on which is noted the mileage at which the work was last done, or the mileage at which it should next be done. It is a matter of personal preference which scheme you adopt, but don't get the figures mixed up. Mark it boldly "Greased at x miles" or "Next oil change at x miles."

A word of warning, here, about grades of oil and greases. Your handbook lists certain grades of lubricant which should be used, and this is reproduced in the appendix to this book. The manufacturers do not pick these names out of a hat; nor do they suggest them because they get a "rake-off" from the oil companies. They don't!

The factory and the research departments of the oil companies both carry out long and expensive tests with the various components, using a wide range of oils and greases. The brands which give the best results—longest life with the least wear—are the brands which are eventually recommended. So stick to them, and do not be tempted to use a different grade of lubricant because it is cheaper or because you have read in an advertisement that it has some magical properties. It may well have them, but unless they happen to be the right properties for your particular machine the results may not be as pleasant as you think.

5 Fault Tracing

WHEN a doctor wishes to diagnose a patient's illness he works methodically, listing the various symptoms to build up an overall picture of the complaint. This done, he can identify it and give treatment accordingly.

Exactly the same type of diagnosis has to be made if a scooter engine refuse to work. Obviously there is a fault, some reason why the engine will not work, and before any fault can be cured it must first be located and identified. The search for it must be just as methodical as is the doctor's approach.

If certain requirements are being fulfilled then the engine *must* work. If it is not working, then it follows that one—or more—of these requirements is not being met, and fault tracing boils down to discovering which it is, and why it is not being supplied.

An engine *must* work if the correct charge of fuel-air mixture is being induced into the crankcase, transferred to the cylinder, properly compressed, fired at the right moment, and the residue properly exhausted. Only an obvious mechanical failure could otherwise stop the unit from firing.

Consequently, fault tracing should always begin with an investigation into these five main requirements, and logically it would start with checking the petroil supply by peering into the tank to see that, in fact, there is a supply of fuel available. The next step should then be the equally obvious one of checking that the fuel is turned on and, if the tank level is low, that it is turned to the reserve position.

Once assured that the tank does contain fuel and that the tap is correctly set, the next check on the list is to ascertain whether or not the fuel is reaching the carburettor. It could be prevented by a blockage in the tap, by a blockage in the pipe, by an air lock, by a choked filter, or by a jammed needle valve.

Normally, this initial check will have taken only a minute or so to carry out, but it will have given one of two quite definite answers. Either fuel is reaching the carburettor, or it is not. If it is not, then you have found at least a contributory cause of the trouble, and this should be rectified before proceeding. If it is reaching the carburettor, you can pass on to the next stage which, with a two-stroke, must always be to check the sparking plug, especially if carburettor flooding has occurred.

Where the engine has been badly overflooded, neat fuel will be trapped in the crankcase, and there will be no chance of starting. Take out the plug, drain all fuel from the float chamber, and switch off the petroil. Then open the throttle wide, so that you admit as much air as possible, and turn the unit over on the kickstarter, briskly, about a dozen times. This should eject most of the trapped fuel. If the plug is wet, dry it; if necessary, burn the petroil off by holding the plug in the flame of a cigarette lighter or a match, and then replace it. Connect the H.T. lead, and operate the kickstarter. If the engine then fires, turn on the fuel. If it does not, turn on the fuel, allow a few seconds for the float chamber to fill, and then kick it again. It should then work satisfactorily.

If the initial inspection of the fuel system has brought no obvious fault to light, the next stage of the fault tracing should be switched to the ignition system. This is always a strong suspect with two-strokes, which tend to be very touchy indeed about their sparking plugs. So, first of all, remove the plug and examine the gap. Obviously this gap should be clear, but two-strokes can suffer from a condition called "whiskering." Under the influence of heat, metallic particles contained in the fuel tend to weld themselves to the plug electrodes, until they eventually bridge the gap completely. When this happens, of course, no spark occurs, since the high-tension current can follow the easier path to earth provided by the whisker joining the electrodes. A whisker is cleared simply by flicking it away with the blade of a pen-knife or with a feeler gauge. At a pinch, a piece of thin cardboard or a folded piece of paper will suffice. Then give the plug a clean with a wire brush and regap it before replacing it. Persistent whiskering is a sign that something else is wrong too. It can indicate that the wrong grade of plug is fitted, or that the engine is running too hot. This, in turn, points to poor scavenging or a weak mixture, and should suggest that either the exhaust system is becoming choked or that a joint is leaking.

Where inspection of the plug shows the spark gap to be clear and neither over-wide nor too narrow, connect the plug to the H.T. lead and place its metal body in contact with the cylinder. Arrange matters so that you can easily see the gap while operating the kickstarter, and then turn the motor over smartly. A good fat spark should jump across the plug points. Repeat the check several times, and if no spark is obtained substitute a brand-new plug—an essential "spare" which should always be carried—and try again. If the new plug sparks and the old one didn't, the obvious inference is that the plug insulation has broken down, and fitting the new plug in its place should cure the trouble.

If no spark is obtained with the new plug, however, then the trouble lies somewhere between the sparking-plug terminal and the magneto, and a more exhaustive examination will have to be made.

Examine the H.T. lead minutely throughout its length, checking the terminals and inspecting the insulation for signs of cracks or perished areas which could be leading to a short-circuit. If you are doubtful about it, try the effect of substituting a spare length of H.T. lead and retesting with that. Examine all the electrical connexions on the H.T. and L.T. side of machines with an external coil.

Finally, remove the inspection plate and take a look at the contact-breaker points. Open them fully, and see if they are worn or dirty. Clean them by inserting a clean slip of card, close the points lightly on it, and withdraw it against their pressure. Do this two or three times, until the card comes away clean. Then open the points fully again and check the gap with a feeler gauge. If all is apparently in order you have then done all that is possible on the electrical side, so far as roadside checking is concerned. A full ignition test is a garage job.

Complete engine failure for any other cause is unlikely, save in the remote event of all the piston rings being broken following a seizure. Other troubles are more likely to show themselves in reduced performance or in erratic running. One of the likelier causes of a lack of pulling power, for instance, is loss of compression, and it is possible, where this is suspected, to deduce where the fault lies from the way the engine behaves. If the crankcase seals have failed there will be a tendency for the unit to spit back through the carburettor, since extra air will be induced into the crankcase and thus weaken the mixture. Where the head joint is fractured, a characteristic hissing noise may be heard as gas is driven through the gap. In both cases the unit will tend to run hot and this, in turn, aggravates the trouble.

Following a seizure, as we have noted, the rings may have fractured. Or, on an engine which has not been decarbonized regularly, the rings may have "gummed up" in their grooves. This not only reduces both crankcase and cylinder compression, but it also allows oil to be driven from the case into the cylinder. This oil burns, and the resulting smoke issuing from the tail pipe is a good clue to watch for. If at any time you have seized your engine, and immediately afterwards it loses performance and begins to smoke, the only wise course is to stop immediately. The rings have almost certainly been damaged, and any further running could seriously damage the bore. This is especially the case where a ring has broken, for its sharp edges will act as highly efficient cutting tools, and the engine can be ruined.

One puzzling fault is pre-ignition. The engine "pinks" continually—a metallic tinkling sound—and will even continue to run when the ignition is cut. This is caused by carbon deposits in the head becoming red hot and igniting the mixture before the spark occurs. The cure is to decarbonize as soon as you possibly can.

Exactly the same process of elimination has to be followed when tracing faults in the lighting system. Faced with electricity, of course, most laymen simply give it best first time, but in fact electrical work is reasonably straightforward provided that magic word "circuit" is borne in mind. Circuits are the key to electricity. If electricity is present and the circuit is complete then the current *must* flow through it. If electricity is present but is not flowing then it follows that the circuit is not complete.

Faulty circuits are of two types: the open-circuit and the short-circuit. In the first case there is a complete break and the wires on the side of the breakage remote from the electrical source are "dead." In the case of a short-circuit the current is still flowing, but is following a shorter path to earth, as would happen, for instance, if one end of a live lead had become detached from its terminal and had earthed itself on the bodywork.

Obviously, then, the first stage is to find out which wire is affected, and to do this it is necessary to be able to read a wiring diagram. Such a diagram may at first sight appear disconcertingly like a plan of a railway marshalling yard, and oddly enough it is not at all a bad idea to think of it as such. The leads become railway lines, and the current the train which has to pass over them. Remember, though, that one important main line is not shown. This is the earth return, formed by the actual framework of the scooter itself. All the components are connected to this earth, which therefore forms one complete half of the circuit.

To trace, for example, the circuit which lights the tail lamp, take as the starting point the unearthed terminal of the battery. Follow this, on the wiring diagram, as it passes—by way of the rectifier—to the lighting switch. From the switch another lead is taken to the tail bulb. Current then passes through the bulb's filament, and thence to earth. Since the other terminal of the battery is also earthed, a circuit exists as soon as the switch is so operated that its tumbler joins the lead from the battery to the lead to the tail lamp. This circuit runs from the battery terminal to terminal 2 of the switch; through the tumbler to terminal 1 of the switch; thence to the tail lamp and to earth. And the earth return completes the circuit. Where really complicated circuits are involved, it sometimes helps to trace them out individually, placing tracing paper over the wiring diagram and following the various lines until you have a picture of the complete circuit, with all its intermediate "stations" marked.

Having found the circuit the next job is to check it. First, obviously, you have to discover whether any current is flowing or not, and here a test rig helps immensely. One can be made quite simply with a bulb, a bulb-holder, and a length of electrical lead. First, place the bulb-holder against one battery terminal, and then touch the other terminal with the end of the lead. The bulb should light. If not, it shows that the battery is flat, and it will have to be re-charged before you can proceed. Never forget that a flat battery is more likely to be a symptom of the trouble than the cause; there is almost certainly a short-circuit somewhere which has caused the battery to drain itself. It is possible for this to be a short-circuit inside the battery itself, so get the garage to check its condition at the same time.

Once you are certain that the battery is all right you must check each individual lead in the circuit in question, a job made considerably easier by the fact that modern wiring harnesses use wires of distinctive colours for each of the individual circuits. Remember, though, that on the Vespa the battery *must* be disconnected whenever you intend to work on the lighting switch.

So, in the case of the specimen circuit to the tail lamp, you would, having checked first the bulb and then the battery, have disconnected it temporarily while the lighting switch was opened up. The end of the lead would then be freed from its terminal, brought clear, and the battery reconnected. The test rig would then have been applied to the open end of the lead; the holder placed against the lead, the holder wire connected to earth. If the lamp then lit it would show that current was reaching the terminal. Again disconnect the battery, replace the lead you had removed, and remove the end of the tail-lamp lead from the switch. In its place connect the test-rig lead, and earth the holder. Connect the battery and operate the switch. If it lights the bulb the switch has a clean bill of health, and the fault must lie either in the tail-lamp lead or in the lamp itself.

Continue checking, stage by stage, throughout the entire circuit. You may find, for example, that when the test rig is connected to the lamp end of the terminal it will not light the bulb. This shows that the fault lies in the lead itself. It has probably fractured, so it must be traced and inspected minutely. If it is a simple fracture you will find two loose ends. Sometimes a short-circuit can be detected by switching on and shaking the machine. As the broken end earths itself a characteristic crackling of electricity can be heard.

More difficult to locate is an internal fracture, where the insulation is undamaged. Garage men use a test rig fitted with a needle-sharp probe which can be pushed through the insulation at various points until a stage is reached at which the test bulb fails to light. This can literally pin-point the position of the breakage. An alternative is to pull two ways on the lead, at intervals of about three inches, until a section is found which stretches under such treatment. This is the section in which the break has occurred.

Where the suspect lead is a very long one, or is inaccessible, a double check and a temporary repair can be made by connecting the two terminals with an external length of wire. Sometimes, a new lead can be drawn through the conduit by wiring it to the old lead and pulling it through with it.

When repairing fractured leads it is important to ensure that no undue electrical stresses are set up and that the insulation is made good. All joints should be twisted together as neatly as possible—it is even better if they can be soldered—and the new joint must be wound round with insulating tape to make leakage impossible. Any terminals which have been undone must be refitted tightly, and if a soldered joint has failed it *must* be resoldered. It is not sufficient merely to tape it up.

Given patience and a modicum of equipment, there is no reason why the average owner should not be able to trace most faults which can occur either in the engine or in the electrical system. Even when the nature of the failure is such that it is not possible to repair it oneself, it is often possible to provide a temporary cure, or at least to save money by giving the repairer an accurate diagnosis of the trouble.

6 Work on Vespa Engines

As we have already noted, the current Vespa engine is the result of nearly twenty years of continual and painstaking development, and it is therefore one of the most reliable of units. Consequently, there is normally very little work to be done on it, apart from scrupulously carrying out the set routine maintenance which will ensure that it is kept in good trim all the time.

So far as major work goes, the only job which needs to be carried out at regular intervals is decarbonizing. In use, the inside of the combustion chamber, the top of the piston, the cylinder ports and the exhaust system tend to accumulate deposits of carbon. Allowed to build up, these have a deleterious effect on the operation of the engine, so from time to time the unit must be stripped and these deposits cleaned away.

Carbon is, in fact, merely a rather harder form of soot. Just as a chimney, if left unswept, eventually becomes clogged with soot, so an engine could become clogged with carbon. Two-stroke engines, in particular, are particularly susceptible to the ill-effects of carboning. This is due partly to the petroil lubrication system—some oil is inevitably burned in the unit—and to the fact that scavenging of the cylinder has to take place in a relatively short period of time. Any obstruction of the exhaust system, and particularly of the exhaust port and the silencer tail pipe, consequently has a far more serious effect on engine output than would the same degree of obstruction in the exhaust system of a four-stroke engine.

Important though decarbonizing is, nevertheless, it is equally possible to spoil an engine by decarbonizing at too-frequent intervals. Every time an engine is stripped and reassembled the seating of the various components is disturbed, and after rebuilding, the unit takes some hundreds of miles to settle down again. During this period the fuel consumption is usually higher than before, and the performance (if the unit was not really in need of attention when it was stripped) is no better, and may even have deteriorated slightly. Obviously, then, it is essential to be able to judge just when to strip the unit, and when to leave it alone.

Many riders work on a rigid basis of decarbonizing after a set number of miles—3,500 miles is generally considered to be the ideal figure for the Vespa—and this system certainly has its advantages. It means that the unit is stripped for major attention perhaps once every year, giving the owner a chance to examine the condition of the working parts and to take remedial action where necessary before any incipient faults have developed to major proportions. Some riders, however, prefer to use the machine until a fall in performance and a rise in fuel consumption is noted. This may not occur until 10,000 or more miles have been covered.

Of the two, the former is better practice. It is not inconceivable that the engine would still continue to give a satisfactory performance with, say, one ring stuck in its groove, or even cracked. But to run the unit for perhaps thousands of miles in this condition is inviting trouble. It could result in a ruined piston and bore, costing some pounds to replace.

Where the annual mileage is over 5,000 a compromise can be adopted which obtains the best of both worlds with the disadvantages of neither. This is to give the engine two overhauls each year: a top overhaul, during which the piston and rings are inspected but the barrel is not removed; and a complete decarbonization, in which the head, barrel and pistons are removed for cleaning and inspection, and the condition of the big-end and small-end bearings is also checked.

With such a plan of maintenance the unit would be given its top overhaul after 3,000 miles running, and its complete "de-coke" after a further 3,000 miles. The next work would be a top overhaul, the one after that a full decarbonization; the two forms of work alternating until, after some 30,000 miles, it might be thought worthwhile to remove the engine from the machine and strip it completely for a thorough check and the renewal, if necessary, of main bearings and so forth.

A TOP OVERHAUL

Although this is a relatively simple job, you must prepare for it properly. It involves opening up the working parts, so scrupulous cleanliness is essential. Thus, the first job is to remove the "blister" from the scooter, and then to bare the engine itself ready for the work to begin.

Detach the plug lead, and then undo the single-point fixing of the cowling which covers the cylinder. Have a tin of grease solvent handy and, with a stiff-bristled brush (a 1-in. paintbrush is ideal), work solvent between the fins, over the head, and round the underside where the silencer is attached. Make sure that the whole cylinder has been covered, and then wash off with water gently flowed over it with a hose.

Leave the unit to dry while you assemble the rest of your tool kit, some clean newspaper on which to place the parts which have been removed, and a scraper with which to clean off the carbon.

You can, of course, buy scrapers, but it is easy enough to improvise one. Perhaps the best is a stick of hard solder, one end of which is filed down to form a wedge. At a pinch, a wedge can be formed in a stick of hardwood. It is inadvisable, though, to use such a "tool" as a table knife or a blunt screwdriver, since these may inflict scratches which will form a first-rate "key" for later carbon formation.

Remove the sparking plug. With a box-spanner, take off the four head nuts. Ease the washers (one spring washer and one flat washer per stud) off too. The head can then be removed by sliding it along the studs.

Loosen the clip which holds the exhaust system to the cylinder's exhaust stud, and the bolt which supports the silencer. The entire unit can then be pulled away from the engine.

With one hand resting gently on the barrel, and a finger held over the bore, turn the engine over with the starter until the piston comes to the top. You can now clean the crown. Scrape away as much carbon as possible,

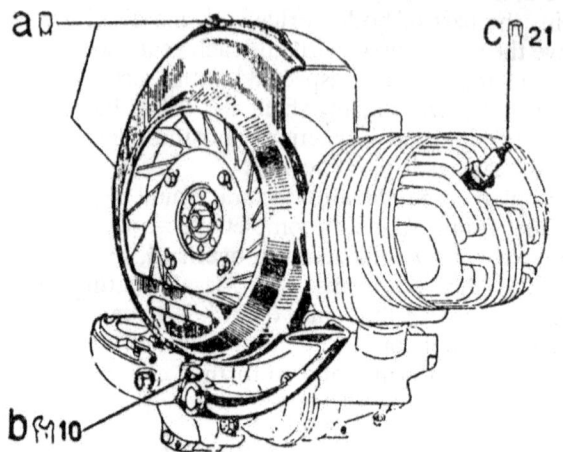

FIG. 9. THE 125 C.C. ENGINE LESS TRUNKING AND EXHAUST PIPE

Fixings for the fan house (*a*) and kickstarter (*b*) are shown. The sparking plug (*c*) is removed before loosening the head bolts. The symbols indicate the type of tool to use and the spanner size.

and finish the job with a wire brush to polish the crown. If you are very careful, and ultra-particular, you can use an abrasive metal polish on the crown too. If you do so, be sure to apply it in such a way that none runs on to the cylinder itself.

Now again press the starter and take the piston down to the bottom of its stroke. This leaves the exhaust port open, and you will be able to work from outside, carefully scraping away any carbon deposit which has formed there. Inevitably, some chips of carbon will fly into the cylinder, so when the port has been thoroughly cleaned these must be removed. In a garage, a few blasts through with a pressure air line does the trick. You may be able to achieve a similar result with a tyre pump. If you are going to use this method, attach the connexion and then give three or four sharp blasts with the pump *before* you take it near the engine. These will clear away any tiny particles of grit which may have accumulated in the pump or connector. You can then safely use it to blow the loose carbon through the still-open exhaust port. If this does not clear it, wash it through with petrol. Since this will also remove the protective oil film on the walls of the cylinder you will have to apply a coating of engine oil afterwards. Wipe it on with your fingers, but make sure they are clean first.

Next it is the turn of the cylinder head. Use your scraper to clear away all the carbon, finishing off with a wire brush. Again, the hypercritical will finish the job with carefully applied metal polish. When working on the head, however, don't overlook the importance of clearing away any carbon which has accumulated round the sparking plug hole or in the threads

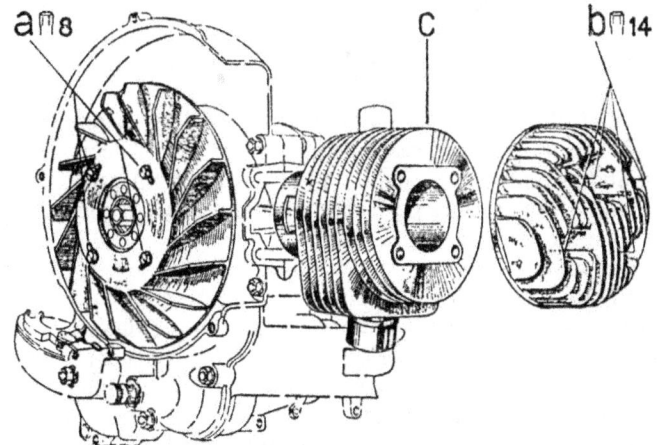

FIG. 10. THE HEAD IS HELD BY FOUR NUTS, SHOWN AT (*b*)
When the nuts have been removed, the barrel (*c*) can be drawn off its studs. If the fan is to be removed, first straighten the tab washers on the holding-down bolts (*a*).

themselves. If left, such a deposit can become incandescent as the engine warms up, leading to pre-ignition of the charge.

Finally, don't forget the plug itself. Modern plugs are not of the type that can be dismantled for cleaning, and the only really effective way is to have it sand-blasted at a garage. After sand-blasting, a plug must always be thoroughly freed of fine grains of sand by a few further blasts of clean air; so make sure this is done. Have the plug gapped as well before you refit it.

Using a new head gasket, replace the cylinder head, the plain and spring washers, and the nuts. Bring each nut to finger tightness, and then lock each down a few turns at a time with your spanner. This ensures that the head is drawn evenly on to the barrel, with no undue local stresses set up.

You can now turn your attention to the silencer. This cannot be dismantled for cleaning, but examination of the tail pipe will give you a clue as to its condition. If any carbon is present in the tail pipe, scrape it away, and do the same to any which you find in the exhaust pipe. If it is suspected that the silencer is choked it is possible to loosen the carbon by immersing the complete unit in a hot solution of caustic soda, made up in the ratio of one gallon of water to three pounds of soda. This is a corrosive solution, so when using it you must be extremely careful. *Never* allow it to come into contact with your eyes, and should any splash on to your skin wash it off at once with plenty of water, or a nasty burn may result. The silencer too, after treatment, will need to be washed. For this, warm water which is slightly soapy is recommended.

Owing to the lack of provision for cleaning, Vespa silencers have a definite "life"—about 20,000 miles is a good average figure—after which they should be replaced. No hard-and-fast rule can be laid down, but a good guide is the note of the exhaust. If this has become uncharacteristically subdued and rather "woolly," then it is time for a new silencer to be fitted.

Replace the silencer and the engine cowling. Then examine the condition of the sparking plug's sealing washer. If it has been squashed flat discard it and fit a new one. This is an important point, since the purpose of this washer is to provide a perfect seal round the plug hole. To do this, it needs to have a certain resilience left in it.

Where a new washer is being used, finger-tighten the plug until you feel it "bite" on the washer. Then apply your plug spanner, and turn the plug body just sufficiently to crush the washer but not to flatten it. Excessive plug tightening can have two serious effects: it can distort the plug body, so causing air leaks and it can strain the threads in the plug hole.

After the machine has been run for about 100–150 miles, it is advisable to make a check on the tightness of all nuts and bolts which have been released, since a degree of bedding-down can take place when the engine is running. Make your check when the unit is still hot after a run.

COMPLETE DECARBONIZING

The basic procedure for a complete decarbonization is similar to that for a top overhaul, save that it is carried several stages further. The engine unit must of course, still be cleaned, but after that the carburettor must be removed and taped out of the way. The head is removed, and the cylinder barrel is slid from its studs. Place one hand beneath the piston as it clears the mouth of the barrel to prevent it dropping on to the studs.

On some machines the cylinder cannot be withdrawn with the engine still in place. Here, the drill is to block up the machine under the footboard and at the rear of the body, and detach the rear wheel, carburettor, and silencer. By removing the bolts which hold the engine to the suspension the engine can be swung downwards and clearance for the barrel obtained. In certain cases, it is simpler still to detach the rear spring and damper, and pivot the entire unit instead of removing the engine bolts.

Place the barrel on your clean newspaper. Then remove the piston. This of course, entails removal of the gudgeon pin, which is secured by a pair of circlips. These are detached, using special circlip pliers (Tool No. T.0017104), although if you are very careful you can spring them out of

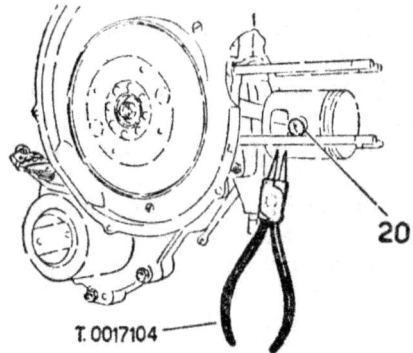

Fig. 11. THE PISTON IS HELD BY THE GUDGEON PIN

To remove the gudgeon pin it is necessary to displace one circlip (20) on each side. Use special circlip pliers for this.

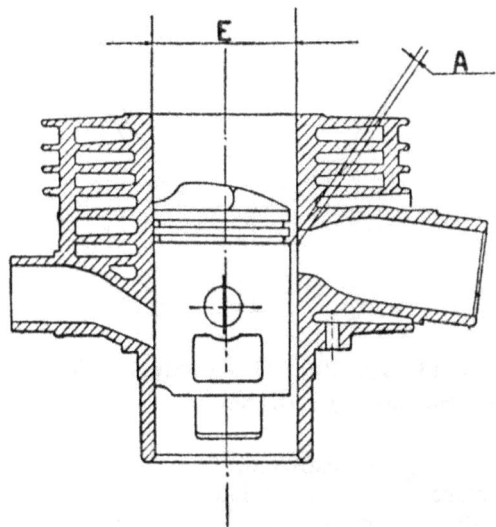

Fig. 12. THE PISTON MUST HAVE A WORKING CLEARANCE IN THE BORE

The maximum clearance is 0·018 mm. When decarbonizing, ensure that the exhaust port, shown here in section, is thoroughly clean.

place with the aid of a fine-bladed screwdriver. The gudgeon pin is then driven out with a shouldered drift (Tool No. 0017820). Again, with care, a plain soft-metal drift can be employed instead.

Now spring the piston rings out of their grooves. Hold the piston in both hands, with your thumbs on the ends of the top ring, facing you.

Gently expand the ring—be careful here; it is made of cast iron, and is very brittle—until it can just be lifted out of its groove and pressed gently upwards and detached. Then do the same with the lower ring, only in this case take it down the piston to avoid the tricky job of manoeuvring it over the top ring groove.

Scrape all carbon from the piston crown, and from the underside of the piston too. Clean out the ring grooves (a piece of broken piston ring makes an excellent scraper for this job) and scrape the inner sides of the rings themselves. Do not, under any circumstances, attempt to scrape their working surfaces. Over the miles these have taken on a fine polish, and

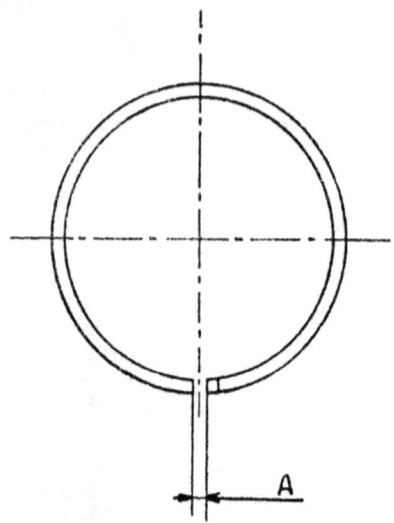

Fig. 13. The Ring Gap is Most Important
The dimension A on a used ring should not exceed 2 mm.

this could all too easily be destroyed. Once you are satisfied, spring the rings back into place. Don't forget that they must match with their pegs.

Examine all cylinder ports for signs of carbon, and scrape them clean, finishing off by polishing with a wire brush. Clean the head, as already described.

Before reassembling, look inside the crankcase and test the big-end for play. To do this, hold the connecting rod and bring it to the top dead centre position. Then try alternately pressing and pulling on the rod. You should be able to feel no up and down movement. If the rod does move, perhaps to the accompaniment of a faint clicking sound, it indicates that the big-end bearing is developing play and will soon need to be replaced.

To rebuild the unit, refit the piston to the connecting rod (the steeper sides of the deflector face upwards) and smear a film of oil round the inside of the bore. With the piston at T.D.C. slide the barrel on to the studs, closing the top ring so that its ends butt on to the peg as you do so. Gently ease the mouth of the barrel over the ring, and then compress the lower ring in turn and slide the barrel fully home.

This done, continue the rebuilding of the engine as for a top overhaul. When carrying out a complete decoke, it is advisable to fit new gaskets throughout as a matter of course. If your machine is one of the latest 150 c.c. models, bear in mind that the cylinder base gasket has been altered and is now of aluminium instead of paper. This change has been introduced to give a better spread of heat throughout the engine by allowing some of the heat to pass from the barrel to the crankcase.

If you have been at all dubious about the compression of your engine, you could take this opportunity of checking the ring gap. When the rings have been removed from the piston and cleaned each, in turn, is inserted into the barrel, at a point about an inch from the top, and is set squarely so that the gap can be measured with a set of feelers. The gap should be 2 mm at the most. If it is more, discard the rings and fit new ones.

7 Major Work on Engine-Transmission Units

ALTHOUGH for the majority of owners, work on their scooter's engine-transmission unit will stop short at routine maintenance and the periodic "de-coke," a knowledge of the make-up of the rest of the internal mechanism is essential if the best is to be obtained from the machine. In addition, even though it is not intended to carry out such jobs as complete removal and dismantling, a thorough understanding of the unit is invaluable if you are called upon to diagnose a fault and to decide whether it is one you can tackle yourself, or whether it should be referred to a fully-equipped Vespa agent. The time spent studying the section devoted to your particular model will, therefore, be well spent.

125 c.c. 152 L2 MODEL

First remove the rear wheel, using a 22-mm box-spanner to take off the four nuts. To detach the wheel from the brake drum remove the two screws which hold the drum to the flange.

Now lay the machine on its side on a suitable bed of sacking. Undo the clutch cable adjuster (8-mm spanner) and the clamp of the rear brake cable (11-mm spanner) and disconnect the cables. Lift the scooter upright, and remove the air cleaner and its rubber bellows, the choke control cable (which is unhooked from the lever on the air cleaner), the throttle cable complete with the throttle slide, and the fuel pipe.

Remove the cover of the low-tension terminal on the rear of the fan casing and disconnect the leads. With an 8-mm spanner disconnect the twin gear control cables. Free the bolt which secures the rear hydraulic damper to the unit, and then use a 24-mm box- or socket spanner to remove the engine anchorage bolt from the frame, just below the cylinder head. The complete unit can then be lifted away from the frame and placed on the workbench.

Remove the cylinder cowling and the fan-housing cover. Release the kickstarter clamp bolt (10-mm spanner) and draw the lever from its shaft. Take out the sparking plug, release the three 14-mm cylinder head nuts, and take off the head and the barrel. Then take off the piston.

Select third gear, remove the two 11-mm nuts holding the gear selector casing, and pull this from the unit.

Flywheel Magneto. Holding the flywheel steady with Tool No. 0013964 undo the nut securing the magneto flywheel, with a 14-mm box-spanner.

MAJOR WORK ON ENGINE-TRANSMISSION UNITS

A circlip is built into the assembly so that undoing the nut automatically pulls the flywheel from its shaft.

The magneto stator plate is now bared, but before proceeding, scribe a mark on the plate and a matching mark on the crankcase. This will enable you to replace it in its correct position with no danger of "losing" the

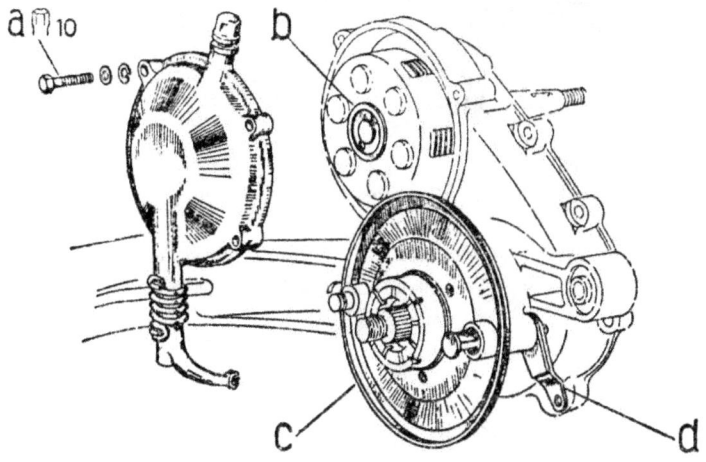

FIG. 14. REMOVING THE CLUTCH

The cover (*a*) hides the clutch, in the centre of which (*b*) is a centralizing plate. This must be lifted out before the clutch can be dismantled. When dismantling the brake, the back plate (*c*) is held by three screws, and the operating arm (*d*) by a split pin.

timing. Undo the screws holding the stator plate, and withdraw it (complete with its sparking plug lead) from the crankcase.

Clutch Removal. On the opposite side of the unit the clutch cover is secured by 10-mm bolts. On the clutch centre is a centralizing plate, which should be operated with a screwdriver to permit the circlip to be removed.

Two tools are required for clutch removal: the C-spanner (Tool No. T.0019354) used to prevent the clutch from rotating, and the special centre-nut spanner (T.0019353). Without these it is impossible to remove the sunken clutch centre nut. The clutch unit will come away, complete with its Woodruff key, when the nut has been removed. To dismantle it a further tool is required, T.0020322. This is placed through the clutch centre, and its wing nut is tightened to compress the clutch springs. When this has been done the large circlip which is fitted in the groove in the rear periphery of the clutch body can be removed. The tool's wing nut is then gently slackened until the spring tension has been released. It is then removed, and the clutch plates and springs can be lifted out. It is also used for reassembly. When fitting relined clutch plates, make sure that the

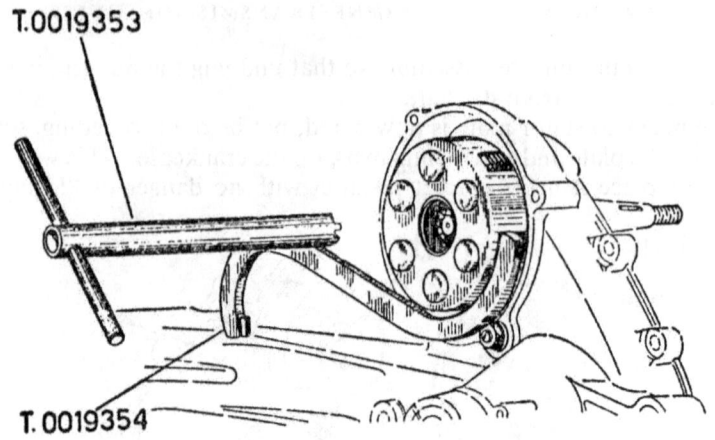

Fig. 15. Two Tools Essential for Removal of the Clutch
One holds the body still, while the other undoes the deeply-recessed clutch centre nut.

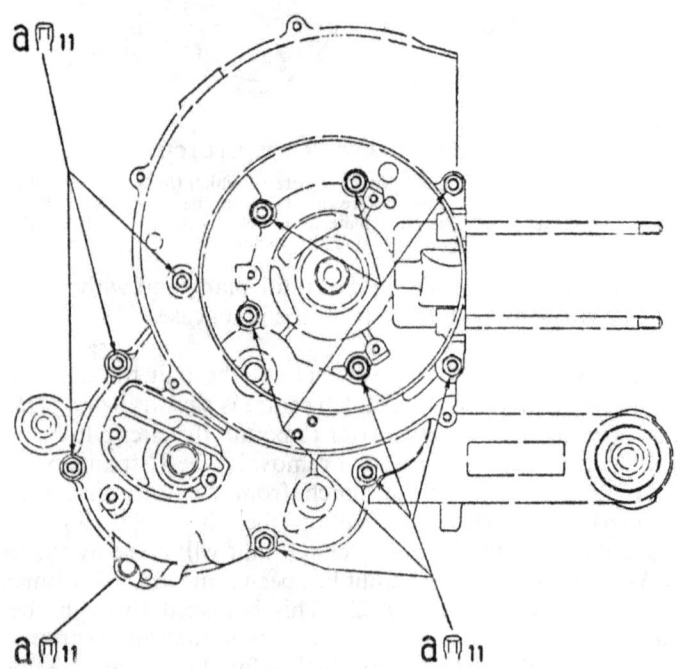

Fig. 61. The Location of the Bolts Which Secure the Two Halves of the Crankcase

MAJOR WORK ON ENGINE-TRANSMISSION UNITS 43

convex side of the outer plate *faces* the cork lining, with the reference mark clearly visible after assembly.

Further Dismantling. Any further dismantling of the engine calls for the use of a number of special tools and for an above-average amount of mechanical know-how. It is therefore advisable to entrust the rest of the work to a Vespa agent. Briefly, however, the procedure is to unscrew the 10 crankcase bolts, using an 11-mm box- or socket spanner and then to fit the special tool to the engine. Tool No. T.0020877/14 is held to the crankcase half on the flywheel side by three screws, and its associated wedge (No. 0017802) is inserted through the crankcase mouth and fixed between the crankshaft webs. A drip tray is set below the unit to catch oil as it is

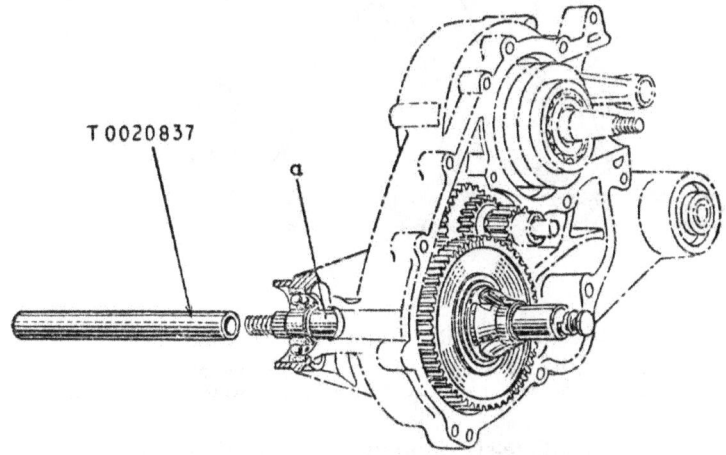

FIG. 17. TO REMOVE THE MAINSHAFT
After splitting the crankcase a special tubular drift is needed.

released, and the tool's central screw, which bears on the crankshaft, is then slowly turned to draw the crankcase halves apart. With the flywheel half of the case will come the entire starter unit.

The Gearbox. This same operation bares the gearbox main shaft and lay shaft. To remove the mainshaft, complete with the gear selector mechanism, a tubular tool (T.0020837) is inserted from the opposite side of the case end is gently tapped. If, therefore, it is your intention to work on the gearbox you should, after the initial work of removing the wheel, also take off the brake drum, using Tool No. 0021084 to undo the centre nut.

To dismantle the gear cluster, hold the shaft in a vice, using pads of soft metal between the jaws and the shaft, and with a pair of circlip pliers (Tool No. T.0017104) release the circlip carried in the groove alongside the low-gear pinion. Then draw the gears off the shaft.

The layshaft and the cush-drive assembly is held by a nut on the clutch side of the crankcase. This shaft runs on needle-roller bearings, and care must be taken not to lose them. In all, there are 23 rollers in the assembly.

Rebuilding. When assembling the gearbox, the layshaft–cush drive needle rollers are held to their track by a thin layer of grease. The assembly is then offered up to the case, and the securing nut is replaced and screwed down.

The mainshaft is drawn into position with Tool No. T.0018119, and the gears are refitted. The smallest pinion goes on first, the largest last. The

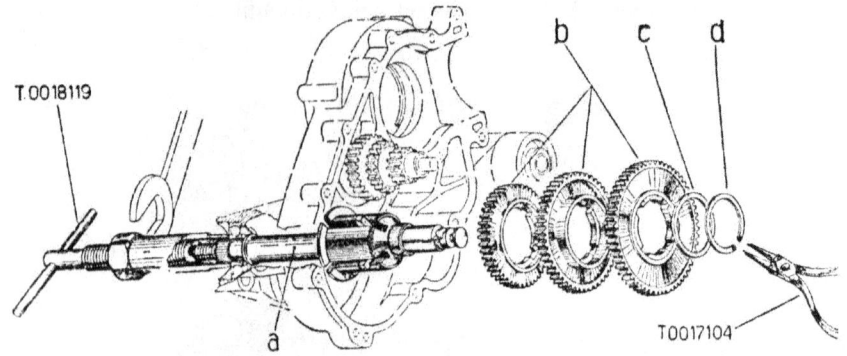

Fig. 18. Replacing the Mainshaft

This calls for the use of a special tool to draw it into place. The gears (*b*), shoulder washer (*c*) and circlip (*d*) are then assembled to the shaft.

small and intermediate-sized pinions are positioned with their collars outermost, but the largest pinion (that for bottom gear) is fitted so that its most pronounced collar points towards the clutch half of the case. The shoulder washer and circlip are then refitted. A feeler gauge should be used to check the play between the top-gear pinion and the shoulder on the shaft. On assembly this should be between 0·15 and 0·30 mm. After use, it should be no more than 0·50 mm. Shoulder rings are available in four oversizes to allow this tolerance to be adjusted as required.

The starter assembly is refitted to the flywheel side of the case. Assemble the starter pinion to the gear cluster so that the pinion's side teeth mesh with the corresponding teeth of the cluster. Check that the two rubber buffers provided for the sector are not damaged. If they are, replace them and ensure that they do not stand out beyond the joint surfaces of the crankcase halves.

The tab of the kickstarter spring is located in the slot in the sector boss and the free end anchored in the hole in the crankcase.

When joining the crankcase halves both must be clean, and a new gasket must be used and smeared with shellac. To guide the engine mainshaft a pilot tube (Tool No. 0017831) is fitted to the flywheel-side shaft, and a special wedge is again inserted between the crankshaft webs. The crankcase halves are then joined together, and the kickstarter is depressed until the sector engages with the starter pinion. The various bolts etc. are next

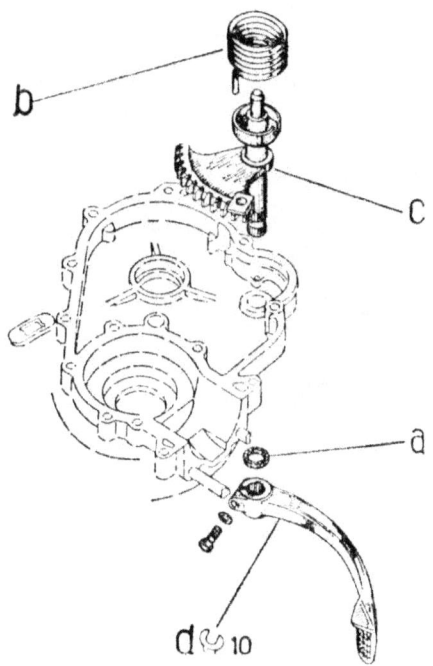

Fig. 19. Reassembling the Kickstarter Mechanism

Parts shown are the shaft and sector (c), return spring (b), spacer (a) and lever (d). The free end of the spring is anchored in a hole in the casing, and final positioning of the lever is made when the unit has been remounted on the machine.

replaced and tightened and the wedge is then removed. Check that the shaft revolves freely.

Jointing compound is applied to the gasket between the crankcase and the gear-shift case, and the selector stem is operated to engage first gear. The shift unit is rotated to third-gear position, the lever's skid is placed in the stem track, and the unit is slipped on to the securing studs and pressed against the crankcase.

Next the mainshaft is turned so that the selector engages in third gear. The case can then be secured and bolted down.

Final Assembly Work. Much of the remaining work is simply a reversal of the dismantling procedure. Refit the clutch, not forgetting its Woodruff

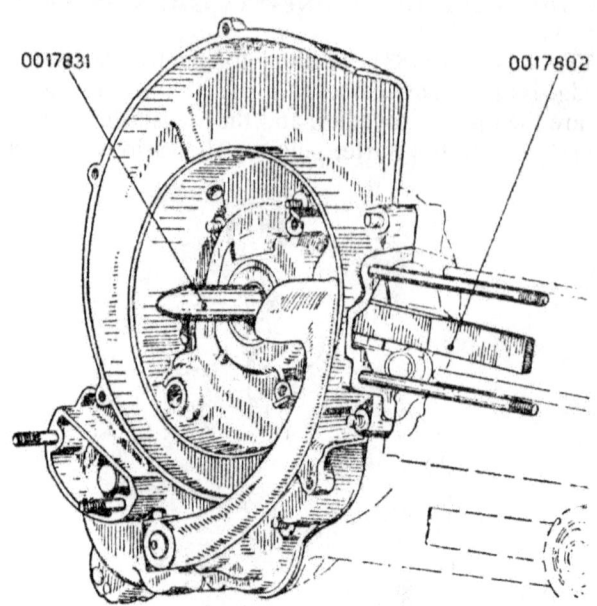

FIG. 20. SPECIAL TOOLS ARE NEEDED TO REALIGN THE CRANKCASE HALVES BEFORE ASSEMBLY

A wedge is used to protect the crankshaft, and a pilot sleeve guides the flywheel-side mainshaft.

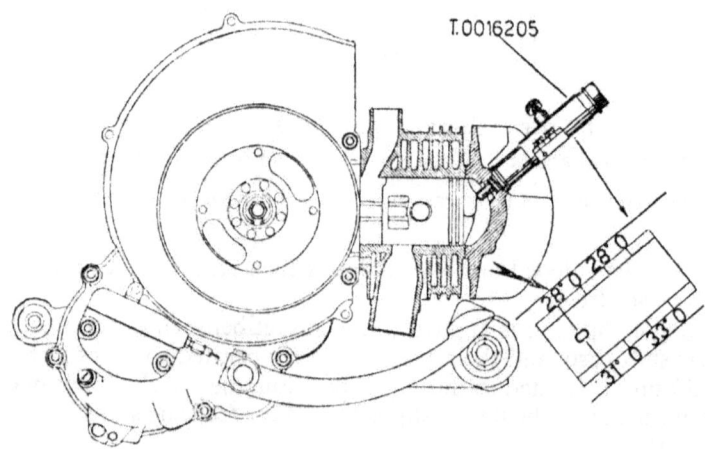

FIG. 21. USING THE SPECIAL TIMING TOOL FOR THE ENGINE

The piston is set to T.D.C. and the zero marks on the inner and outer rods of the tools are aligned. Degree readings can then be taken accurately and the points set.

key, and then the piston, barrel and head. Replace the stator plate, lining up the marks which have previously been scribed on the plate and the case.

If, however, the timing has been lost, the procedure to follow is this. Refit the flywheel and bring the piston to T.D.C. Insert Tool No. T.0016205 in the plug hole and line up the zero mark on its outer sleeve with the line on the inner rod. Rotate the flywheel, anti-clockwise, through 90°, and then turn it back again, watching through the flywheel slots for the exact moment of opening of the contact-breaker points. They should break at 28° before T.D.C. If the ignition is incorrectly set, remove the flywheel, loosen the clamping screws on the stator plate, and turn it by the appropriate amount—clockwise if the ignition is too far advanced; anti-clockwise if it is retarded. Tighten the screws, replace the flywheel, and repeat the check until the timing is correct. In the absence of the correct tool, a timing disc with suitable cutaways can be used instead.

ROTARY-VALVE MODELS—125 c.c., 150 c.c. STANDARD AND 150 c.c. SPORTIQUE RANGE

All these machines employ the ingenious rotary-valve engine which was introduced on scooters with the VBA frame prefix, distinguishing them from the earlier VB 1 "150s" which were fitted with conventional three-port engines. On the Sportique versions, a four-speed gearbox is fitted. The general mechanical layout is, however, similar for all machines.

Engine Removal. Disconnect the clutch control cable by releasing the adjuster screw from the abutment on the underside of the crankcase (8-mm spanner) and then release the clamp on the rear brake cable (11-mm box- and 8-mm open-ended spanner). Screw the cable adjuster from its housing (8-mm spanner) and unscrew the clip retaining the gear-change control cables to the crankcase casting. It is held by a nut, for which an 11-mm box-spanner is needed.

Remove the blister cowling from the bodywork and take off the single screw holding the gear index-plate case cover. With an 8-mm spanner unscrew the adjusters of the gear control cables and detach the cables themselves. Take off the air cleaner cover, held by one screw, and the bolt which holds the hydraulic rear damper. For this a 14-mm box-spanner and a 14-mm open-ended spanner are required.

Disengage the throttle control cable nipple from the end of the throttle slide control rod—an 8-mm spanner is needed—release the choke cable from the choke-valve lever by sliding it from its seating. Take off the rubber bellows connecting the air cleaner to the intake, detach the fuel hose (10-mm spanner) remove the bolt holding the engine to the frame (22-mm box-spanner). Straighten up the spindle and remove it with the liner. Remove also, the damper spindle. Then slip the engine unit out of the frame.

Detach the silencer (11-mm box- and 14-mm open-ended spanner), undo the four 22-mm wheel nuts and the two screws which hold the brake drum, and remove the centre nut with Tool No. T.0021084.

Engine Dismantling. With the engine on the bench remove the carburettor–air cleaner casing (11-mm box-spanner). Take off the cowling. Detach the fan cowling, undo the 10-mm clamp bolt which holds the kickstarter pedal, and ease the pedal off its shaft. Then remove the fan. The bolts securing this are locked by tab washers, which must first be straightened.

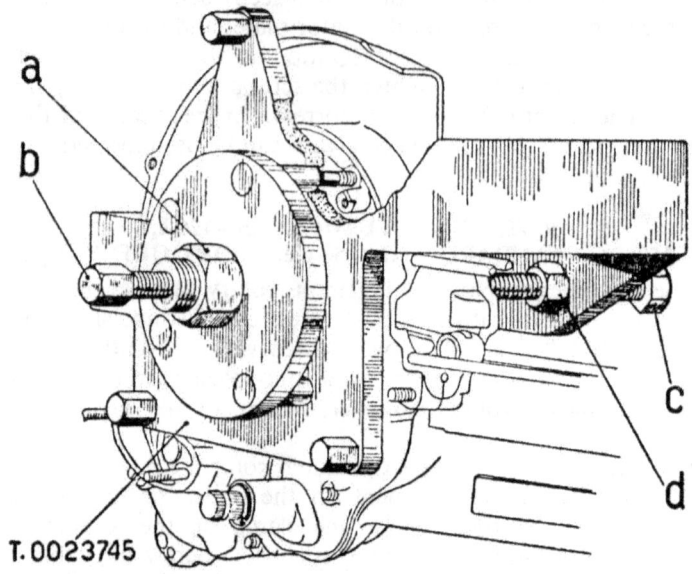

FIG. 22. THE SPECIAL TOOL REQUIRED TO SPLIT THE CASES

Nut *c* is locked against the drive-side mainshaft with nut *b*. Nut *a* presses the plate against the timing side case, and bolt *b* drives the crankshaft from position.

Subsequently use an 8-mm box-spanner on the bolts themselves. Detach the cylinder head (11-mm box-spanner) and slide the barrel off its studs, supporting the piston as its clears the bore.

Select third gear, and then release the 11-mm nuts holding the gear index-plate casing to the gearbox. Remove the circlips from the piston's gudgeon pin bosses, and drive out the pin with the special drift (0017820). Slide the needle cage out of the small end of the connecting rod.

Holding the flywheel steady with Tool No. 0013964 use a 14-mm box-spanner to undo the centre nut. The flywheel will draw off as you do so.

Now remove the external ignition coil, the stator (held by the three screws passing through the slots in the periphery of the plate) and the associated wiring. To guard against accidental demagnetization place the

MAJOR WORK ON ENGINE-TRANSMISSION UNITS

stator inside the flywheel rotor. Before removing this plate, scribe matching marks on the plate and the crankcase to aid reassembly.

Clutch Removal. Remove the 10-mm bolts which hold the clutch cover, and lift this from the unit. Operate the centralizing plate with a screwdriver so that the circlip can be released, then, holding the clutch body with Tool No. T.0019354, undo the centre nut with Tool No. T.0019353. Slide the clutch off its shaft. Stripping the clutch for overhaul, replacing plates,

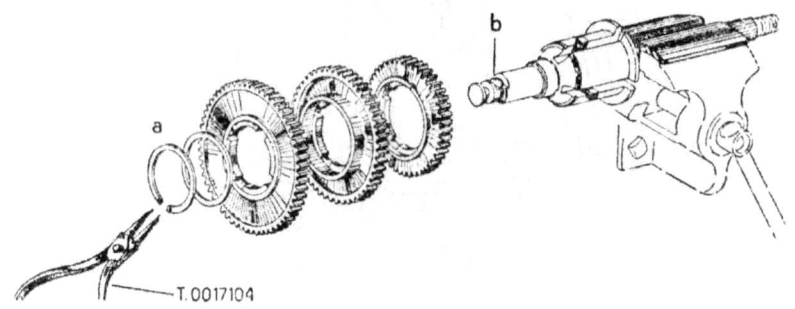

FIG. 23. REMOVING THE MAIN SHAFT GEARS

Circlip *a* is released and the gears drawn off. Selector *b* has a left-hand thread.

and final reassembly of the unit involve the same procedure as that already described for the 125 c.c. model.

Rear Brake Removal. Unhook the brake shoes from their pivots. Then remove the split pin on the operating lever shaft, release the lever and pull out the cam. Remove the back plate.

Further Dismantling. Stripping to this stage is probably the most that a private owner would wish to do. Further work requires a number of special tools, and a degree of mechanical "know-how." The main outlines of the subsequent work are, however, given here for the benefit of owners who wish to work on their gearboxes or on the crank assembly. It should be stressed, however, that to attempt to do so without the special tools noted here and without the appropriate service manual and data sheets is not to be recommended.

Using an 11-mm box-spanner remove the crankcase bolts. Then fix Tool No. T.0023745 to the flywheel side of the engine, and place an oil tray beneath the unit. On the clutch side of the unit the centre bolt of the tool is screwed in until it contacts the crankshaft, when it is held securely by a lock-nut. On the flywheel side the tool's large nut is then tightened to bring the plate's pins into contact with the projecting studs of the clutch-side crankcase half. Further movement breaks the joint and detaches the clutch-side case. The lock-nut and bolt on the clutch side of the crankshaft are then released, and the bolt on the flywheel side is tightened to press the crankshaft out of the flywheel-side case. During this operation the crankshaft must be supported to prevent it falling and being damaged.

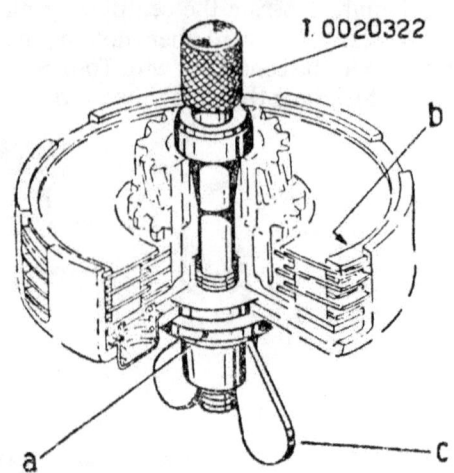

FIG. 24. DISMANTLING THE CLUTCH, USING A SPECIAL TOOL AS A CORE

The shaft (*a*) is placed through the clutch and the wing-nut (*c*) tightened. The circlip (*b*) can then be removed, and the spring tension gradually released.

The kickstarter mechanism will come away with the flywheel-side crankcase half, to which it is held by a circlip.

Dismantling the Gearbox. Further work to dismantle the gearbox entails use of the same tools and the procedure outlined earlier in this chapter in the section dealing with the 125 c.c. Vespa unit.

Reassembly of the Unit. Up to the stage of timing the engine, reassembly is also identical with the procedure advised in the section on the 125 c.c. engine. To refit the unit to the machine, simply reverse the procedure used when dismantling it.

150 c.c. G.S. VESPA

Although this machine retained the same well-tried basic layout employed on the other contemporary models in the range, it differed substantially in detail construction. A four-speed gearbox was used in conjunction with a three-port engine, admission of fuel–air mixture being by means of a piston-controlled port.

Removing the Engine. Block up the scooter so that the rear wheel is clear of the ground. With a 22-mm box-spanner remove the four wheel nuts, and the two screws retaining the brake drum to the flange. Then, with Tool No. 0015309 undo the centre nut on the axle.

The finned locking ring screw securing the exhaust pipe to the stud on the cylinder is undone with Tool No. T.0021214, and a 14-mm box-spanner is employed on the single bolt holding the silencer to the frame. This assembly is then removed from the machine.

An 8-mm open-ended spanner is used to disconnect the clutch cable, an 11/14-mm box-spanner to free the nut on the engine bracket and the retaining carrier of the gear-change control cables. The detachable engine cowling is then released from the bodywork.

Undo the knurled ring on the carburettor mixing chamber and remove the throttle slide and its cable, taping them to the bodywork so that they will not be left dangling, with the danger of being damaged. Remove the rubber bellows and the air cleaner, and with a 14-mm open-ended spanner release the fuel pipe. Free the low-tension cable from its mounting on the body, unlock the ferrules of the twin gear-change cables at the gearbox end, and then undo the twin bolts which hold the engine to its bracket. Support it carefully as you slide it from its mounting and place it on the workbench.

Stripping the Engine. Loosen the clamp which secures the carburettor to its stud and lift it from the unit. Remove the external ignition coil, the plug lead and its rubber grummet (22-mm open-ended spanner and 10-mm box-spanner) and with a 14/10-mm box-spanner remove the various bolts of the cowling from the cylinder. An 11-mm box-spanner should then be used to remove the induction pipe.

Take out the screws securing the fan cover to the crankcase, remove the sparking plug, and then gently straighten out the locking edges of the lock plate on the kickstarter pedal. This done, remove the two 11-mm bolts which hold the pedal.

Unlock the tab washers on the fan bolts, and remove the fan (8-mm box-spanner). With a 14-mm box-spanner undo the cylinder head nuts, slide the head off its studs, and then carefully remove the barrel, supporting the piston as you do so.

The gudgeon pin is retained by circlips, to remove which circlips pliers (Tool No. T.0017104) should be employed. A shouldered drift (Tool No. 0017820) is then used to drive the pin out of the small end.

Holding the flywheel with Tool No. 0013964, remove the centre nut with a 14-mm box-spanner. Removal of this nut automatically draws the flywheel off its shaft. Then use the circlip pliers again to take out the rotor circlip.

A separate fan housing is used on the G.S. Vespa, and it is held by three cheese-headed screws. Ease the housing off the crankcase, and then scribe a mark on the magneto stator plate, and a matching mark on the crankcase. This will enable you to realign the stator, on reassembly, without "losing" the timing. Remove the screws which secure the stator, lift it away, and place it in the rotor so that there is no danger of demagnetizing. Then take out the screws which hold the gear-change toggle. With the toggle, engage second gear. Then fit Tool No. T.0019982 to the starter bush and rotate the bush as far as it will go.

Clutch Removal. Turn now to the clutch side of the unit, and with an 8-mm spanner remove the bolts which hold the clutch cover. Lift this off, and take out the centralizing plate which you will find in the clutch centre.

Fit Tool No. T.0020128 to the clutch body to prevent rotation, and with a 14-mm box-spanner undo the clutch nut. Here, the G.S. differs from all

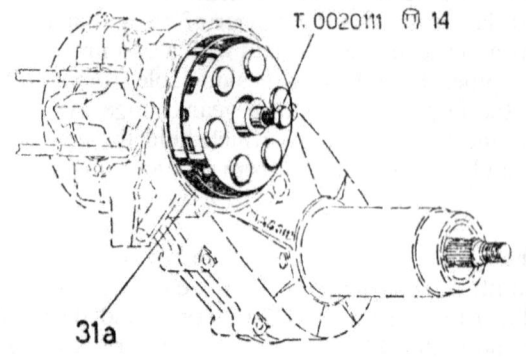

FIG. 25. TO REMOVE THE CLUTCH FROM THE G.S. VESPA
An extractor which draws the complete assembly (31a) off its shaft, is required for this.

other models described in this book. It is not necessary to use a special spanner for the clutch centre nut, but it *is* essential that the extractor (Tool No. T.0020128) be used to draw the clutch from its shaft. It is also necessary to have special tools for stripping the clutch. To remove the plates and springs it must be mounted on Tool No. 0020601 and the threaded ring on the clutch pressure plate must be unlocked with Tool No. T.0020608. Subsequently, proceed on the lines detailed under the appropriate section dealing with the 125 c.c. unit.

Splitting the Crankcase. Release the crankcase bolts (11-mm box-spanner) loosening each a little at a time. Then insert the wedge (Tool No. 0017802) between the crank webs and fix Tool No. T.0020877 to the flywheel side of the crankcase. Tighten its centre bolt progressively to bring pressure to bear on the crankshaft and thus separate the two halves of the case. While keeping up the pressure, also use a hammer to tap a soft-metal drift against the abutment on the lower edge of the gearcase, working from the clutch side.

MAJOR WORK ON ENGINE-TRANSMISSION UNITS

Stripping the Gearbox. When the case parts, the flywheel side will come away, leaving the crankshaft, layshaft and mainshaft in place in the clutch-side case. Using a pair of circlip pliers take off the circlip on the low-gear pinion and ease the gears off the shaft. The shaft itself can be driven out by inserting Tool No. 0020837 on the brake-nut end of the shaft and jarring it out from the clutch side. Before doing so turn the mainshaft so that its longest slot faces the cush gear assembly.

Since the tool for removing the crankshaft locks on to the nut holding the layshaft–subgear assembly the crankshaft should be pressed out next.

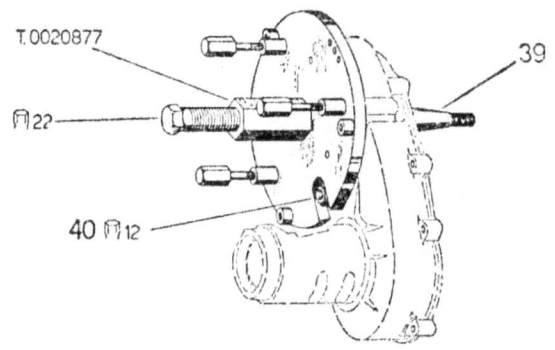

FIG. 26. USING A SPECIAL SERVICE TOOL TO DRIVE OUT THE G.S. CRANKSHAFT (39), COMPLETE WITH BEARINGS
The tool locks on to the nuts of the cush drive (40).

Assemble the tool (No. T.0020877) on the clutch side of the unit and tighten its centre bolt to press the crank out of the case. Then release the shaft's 12-mm nut and remove it from its housing. The starter ratchet and the starter assembly remain in place in the flywheel-side crankcase half. The ratchet can be lifted out, but the assembly itself is secured by a circlip. When this is removed and the screw retaining the slotted starter bush is taken out of the boss of the starter casting (11-mm box-spanner), the assembly can be driven out with a sharp blow from a hide-faced mallet.

Reassembling the Gearbox. Insert the layshaft into the cush drive. Place the 23 needle-rollers of the layshaft bearing into their housing, holding them in place with a film of grease, and refit the layshaft assembly. Draw the mainshaft into place with Tool No. T.0018119 and turn the shaft so that the longest slot faces the cush drive. Refit the gears as described in the section dealing with the 125 c.c. machine. If the starter assembly has been removed press it back into place with the aid of Tool No. T.0020168. This job may be eased if the alloy case is warmed to expand the housing slightly.

Rebuilding the Engine. Refit the crankshaft, clean the joints of both crankcase halves, smear a new gasket with shellac, and place it on the clutch-side half. Offer up the flywheel half of the case, insert the crankcase bolts, and tighten them evenly. Refit the clutch assembly, align the stator

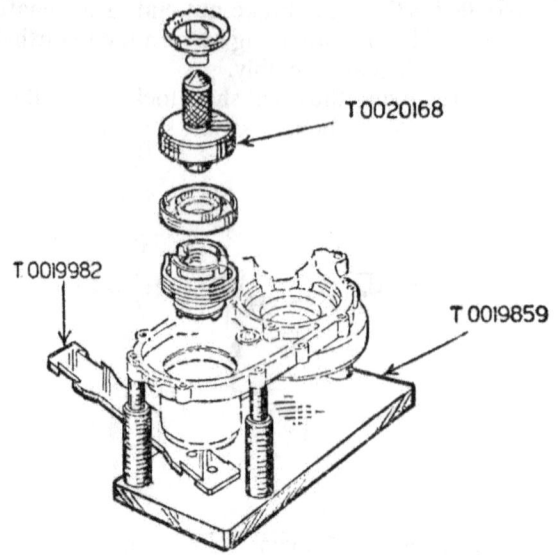

FIG. 27. BEFORE THE STARTER ASSEMBLY CAN BE REINSERTED IN THE CASE ITS HOUSING MUST BE WARMED TO EXPAND THE METAL
A special tool is then used to drive it into place.

plate with the mark previously scribed on the crankcase, lock down its screws, and replace the flywheel.

If the timing has been lost, proceed as advised in the section on the 125 c.c. engine, but remember that with the G.S. unit 31° of advance are allowed.

The remainder of the rebuilding is simply a reversal of the original dismantling procedure.

LATER MODELS, 150 c.c. G.S. VESPA

In the preceding section, the details given refer to the earlier models of the Vespa G.S.—the Model VS 2, VS 3, and VD 2 T.S.

Later versions of the machine differed in a number of points. On the VS 4 series several modifications were introduced, mainly to the cycle parts and the bodywork.

The engine cowling lock was changed and different wheel rims were fitted. Internally, the transfer ducts were ground so as to give a better power output, and metal wadding in the air cleaner was replaced by a plastic material.

For a number of engine jobs new tools were brought in, but the older tools were still usable. Subsequent to the VS 4, the VS 5 was introduced with further modifications. The wheels were different in design and these were secured to the light alloy brake drums by five studs. At the rear, the driving flange and rear brake drum were made in a single unit, and consequently the four wheel nuts were no longer fitted.

Consequently, before starting work on a Vespa G.S. it is essential to check the frame and engine numbers to make sure to which series it belongs. This is also essential when ordering spares for these models.

When timing the G.S. Vespa, it should be noted that models subsequent to Serial No. VS 5 T.0069272 have a higher compression ratio, and that, in consequence, the timing on these machines has also been altered. Instead of the points opening 31° B.T.D.C. they must open 27° B.T.D.C.

8 Electrical Equipment

EACH machine has two totally distinct electrical circuits: that for the ignition, and the circuit which provides current for lighting and the horn. Of these, it is the ignition circuit which you will be called upon to deal with more frequently. The lighting circuit, barring accidental damage, is hardly likely to give any trouble, since it contains no moving parts apart from the switch tumblers.

To obtain the best performance from the two-stroke Vespa engine, however, a careful check must be maintained on the condition and adjustment of the contact-breaker points, and the timing should also be checked at major overhauls, the method to be adopted being that already described in Chapter 7.

The contact-breaker points are located on the stator plate, inside the flywheel, and for adjustment can be reached through the slots in the flywheel face. Adjustment is made by loosening the clamping screw that holds the fixed contact plate and operating the eccentric which can be seen projecting through a slot in the plate. Subsequently, the locking screw is tightenened.

Before making any adjustment, the sparking plug should be removed and the flywheel turned until the points are fully opened. The gap between them should then be accurately measured with a feeler gauge. On 125 c.c. models this should be 0·4 mm (0·015 in.); on 150 c.c. machines 0·3–0·5 mm (0·011–0·019 in.); and on G.S. models 0·4–0·5 mm (0·015–0·019 in.). If the gap falls outside these limits it must be reset.

Contact-breaker points lead a hard life. They may open and close as frequently as 5,000 times each minute, and are subjected to fairly considerable electrical stresses as well. Consequently, they should be inspected for condition at least at each annual overhaul. This is done by removing the flywheel rotor to give free access to the stator plate, and then opening the points so that their contact surfaces can be clearly seen. They must be clean and free from pitting. Where arcing has occurred, a depression may be worn in one point and a corresponding mound built up on the other. Such points must be replaced, since it is impossible for them to work efficiently.

Where the pitting is only skin deep it is usually possible to restore the surface by removing the points and refacing them on a stone. Alternatively most garages would be able to reface them with a dressing machine. Points must also be refaced if they have worn at an angle to each other since to form an efficient switch the contacts must meet and part at right angles.

Cases of premature wear of the fibre heel on the contact-breaker arm, investigated by the manufacturers, have disclosed that some owners do not realize the importance of lubricating the felt pad which oils the cam. This pad is spring-loaded on to the cam, and thus spreads a fine film of oil over it at each revolution of the engine. This ensures that friction between the cam and the heel of the contact arm is kept low. If the pad is allowed

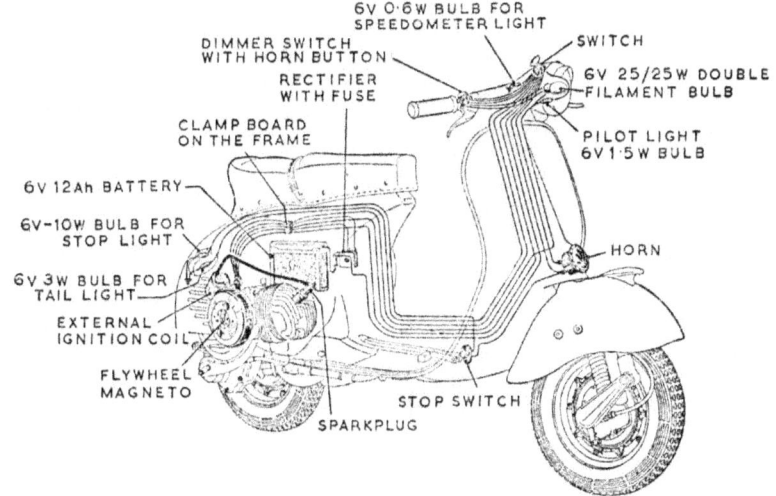

FIG. 28. THE WIRING HARNESS OF A G.S. VESPA SHOWING THE DISPOSITION OF THE MAIN COMPONENTS

to dry out, the cam receives no lubrication, friction between the moving parts is increased, and the heel wears quickly.

When checking the points gap, then, a light should be directed through the access holes and the condition of the felt pad ascertained. It should be well soaked with oil, though not so saturated that excess oil is running off it on to other parts of the magneto. If it requires lubrication the flywheel rotor *must* be removed. The job cannot be done properly by trying to inject oil through the access holes. A light machine oil—not engine oil, which is too thick—should be run carefully on to the pad. It is especially important to carry out this servicing if the machine has been laid up for some weeks.

One puzzling fault which can sometimes occur with flywheel magnetos is demagnetization. When this happens, the strong magnetic field necessary for the production of electricity in the magneto either no longer exists or is sharply reduced, so that only a weak current is obtained.

Demagnetization cannot be cured by the owner, but it can be prevented.

It has been found that, in many cases, the cause of the trouble has been that work had been carried out on the handlebar switch without the battery leads first being disconnected. With the battery still in circuit, it was quite possible for the d.c. lead from the battery to the switch to touch one of the leads from the stator plate. This would allow the battery current to flow along this lead, pass through one of the stator plate coils, and thus cause

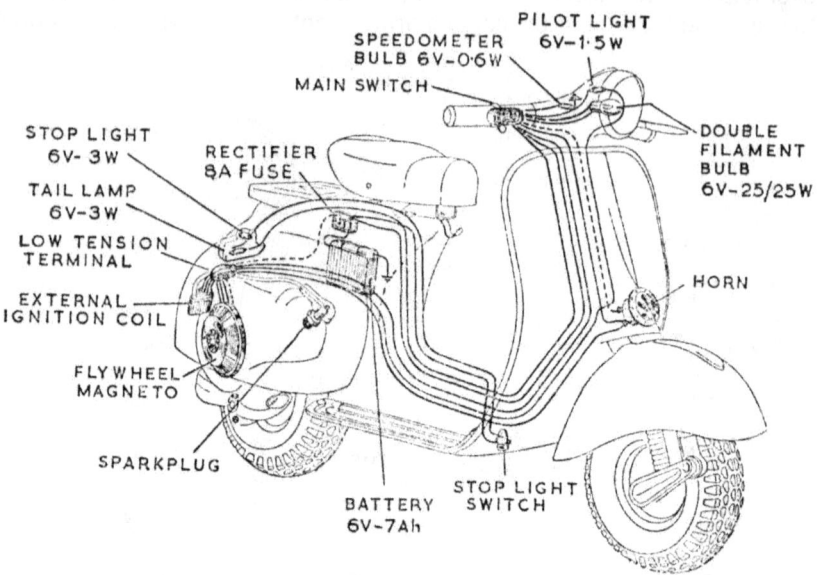

FIG. 29. HOW THE WIRING IS LAID OUT ON THE 150 c.c. VESPA
Dotted lines indicate white cables.

the magnets in the rim of the flywheel to lose their magnetism. Much the same effect can be caused if the leads to the battery are assembled in the reverse of the correct order. The proper connexions are on the wiring diagrams in this chapter, and it is important to study these.

A little care must also be exercised with regard to the battery itself. Several different types are fitted to Vespa scooters. Some of these are of the orthodox wet-cell type, in which the electrolyte is in liquid form. Others are dry-cell batteries, in which a jellified electrolyte is employed.

The dry-type battery is the S.A.F.A. Varley 3V5L. Where this is to be recharged it should be topped up with distilled water before and during charging. After recharging for 24 hours at 0·75 amps all the surplus liquid must be removed.

In normal use, this battery must be removed from the machine for topping up. This should be done *after* a journey, never before one. One teaspoonful of distilled water should be added to each cell and the battery

ELECTRICAL EQUIPMENT

allowed to stand for a quarter of an hour. *All excess moisture must then be removed, either by siphoning it away or by shaking it out.*

Wet-cell batteries of the Lucas PUZ 5E-11 type must have the specific gravity of the electrolyte checked periodically. The hydrometer reading, at 60°F, should be between 1·270 and 1·290. If the battery is put in for

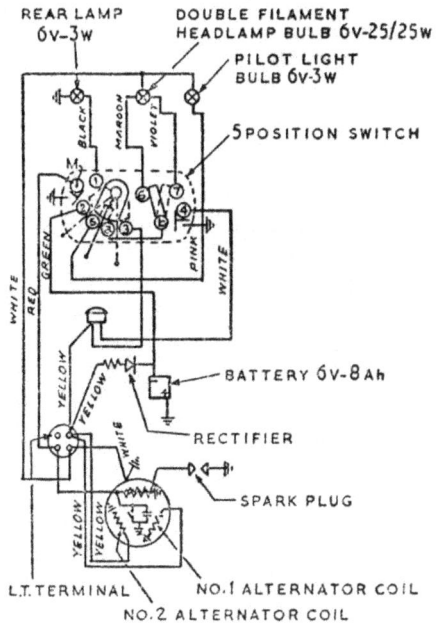

Fig. 30. Wiring Diagram of 125 c.c. Models up to Serial No. 15240

With the switch in position 0 the lights are off; in position 1, contacts 1, 3 (6 or 7), *a* and *b* are connected. Alternating current then flows to the headlamp (main or dipped beam) and the tail lamp. With position 2, selected contacts 1, 2 and 5 are connected, and d.c. current passes to parking and tail lamps.

recharging it is essential that a charging rate of exactly one ampere is specified.

With the S.A.F.A. Type T3V3L the charging rate must not exceed 1·5 amp until each cell returns a voltage of 2·6–2·7 volts, this usually happening after 12 hours. The electrolyte level must be checked monthly, and brought up to the correct amount with distilled water if necessary. Similar instructions apply to the Titano 3P3 battery, save that this must be recharged at 0·7 amps until the cell reading of 2·7 volts is obtained, and during charging its temperature must not exceed 113°F.

In the case of all these batteries, it is important to keep the terminals clean, and to grease them periodically with lanolin. On the S.A.F.A. Varley the connector bars should be lightly greased with this substance.

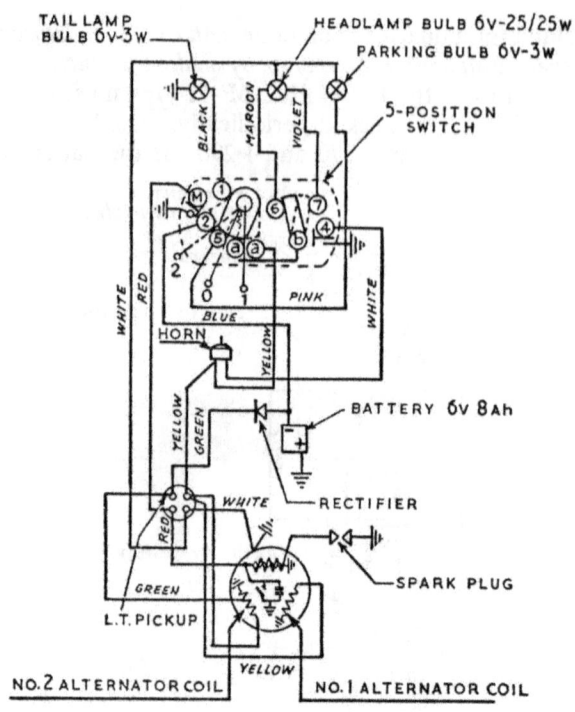

Fig. 31. Equivalent Wiring Circuit for 125 c.c. Machines from Serial No. 15241 Onwards

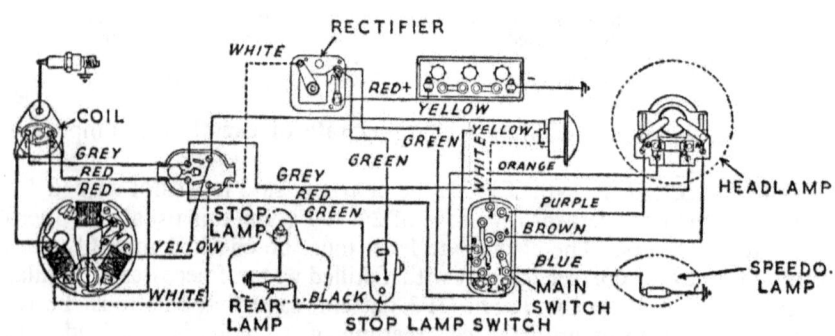

Fig. 32. The Original Wiring Diagram for the 150 c.c. Vespa

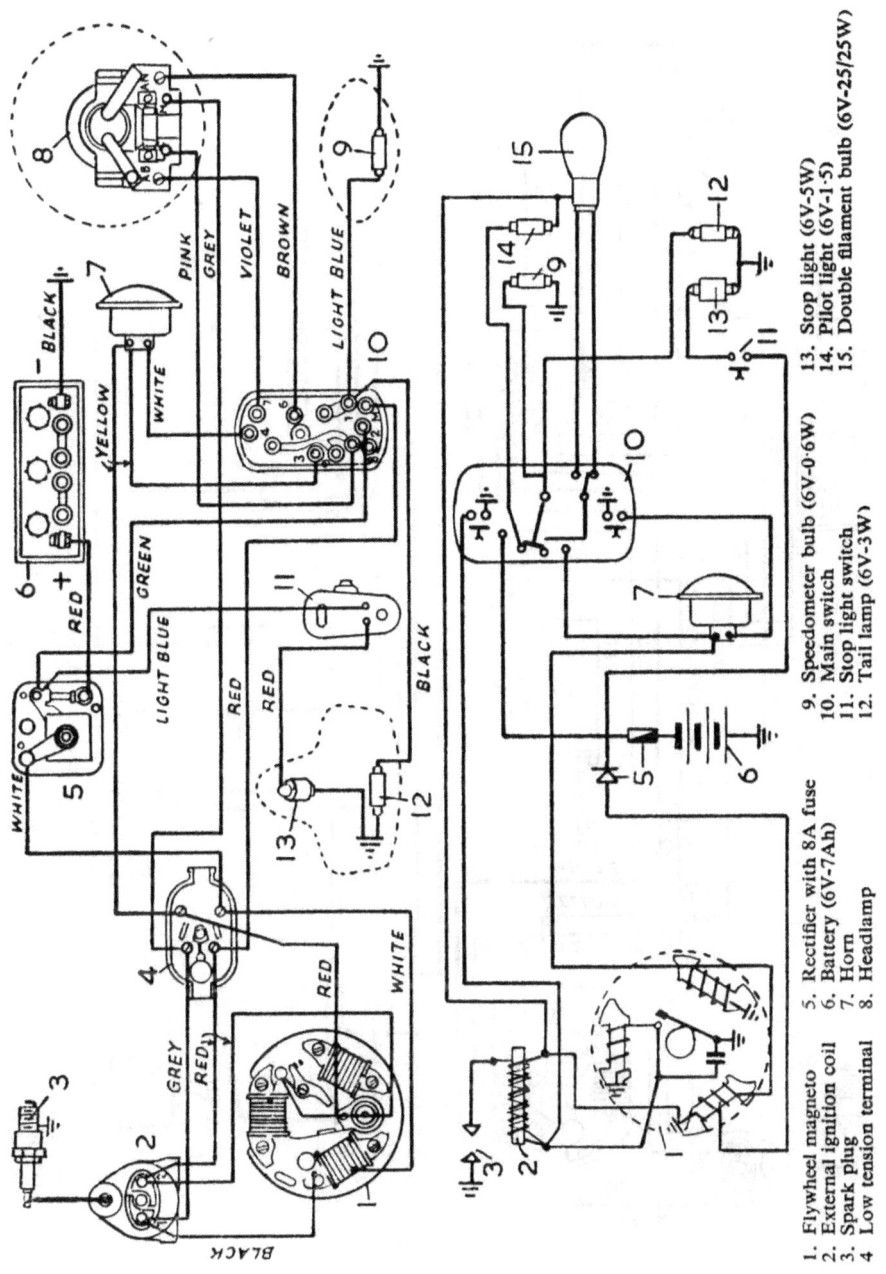

FIG. 33. ONE OF THE TWO 150 VESPA VBA WIRING SYSTEMS
Compare this with the circuit in Fig. 34 which is an alternative for this model.

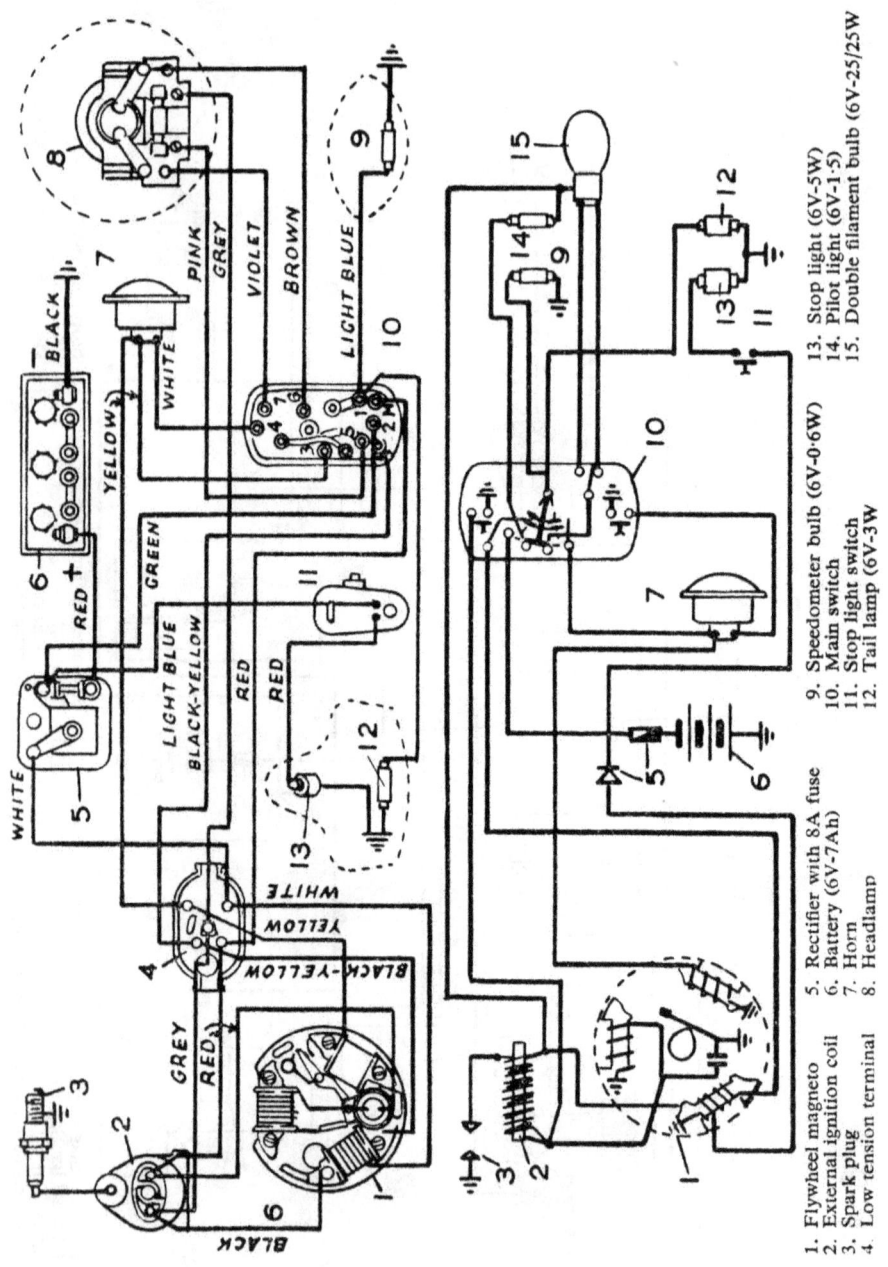

FIG. 34. THE No. 2 CIRCUIT FOR 150 c.c. VESPA VBA MACHINES

In this layout the lighting coils, instead of being connected together at the junction box and sharing a common lead to the switch, have separate leads. An additional terminal (No. 8) in the switch is bridged to No. 3 terminal by a movable contact.

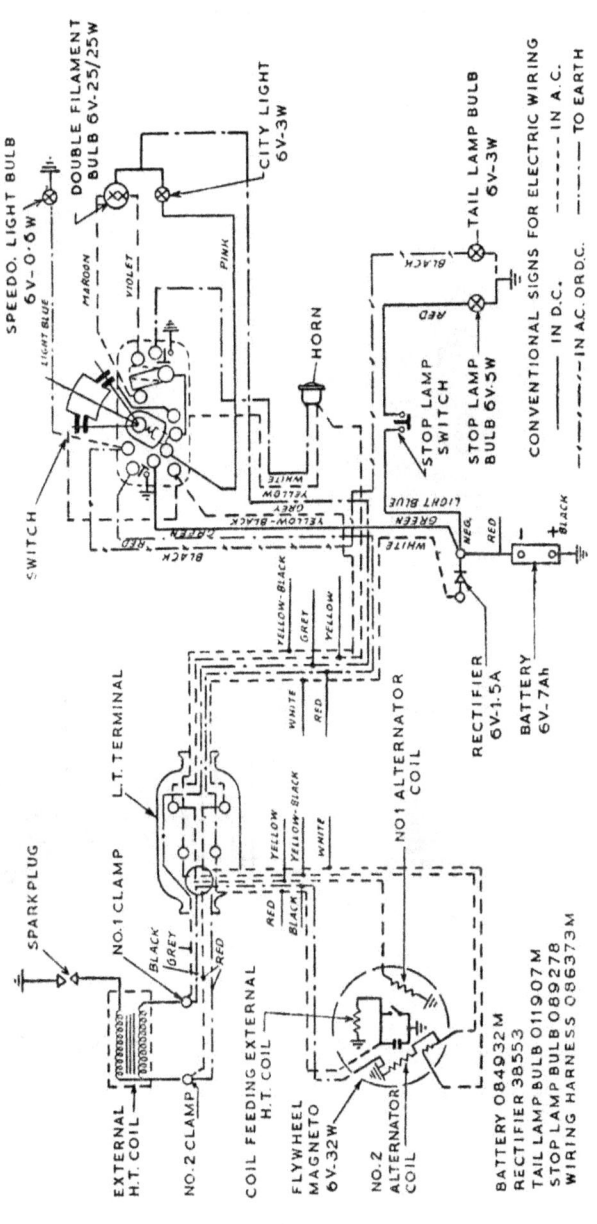

Fig. 35. The Wiring of the 150 c.c. Sportique

With the switch in position 0 the low-tension coil is not in circuit. In position 1, a.c. current passes to the headlamp, tail lamp and speedo bulb. In position 2, direct current is taken to the parking lamps and speedo light. The L.T. coil remains in circuit.

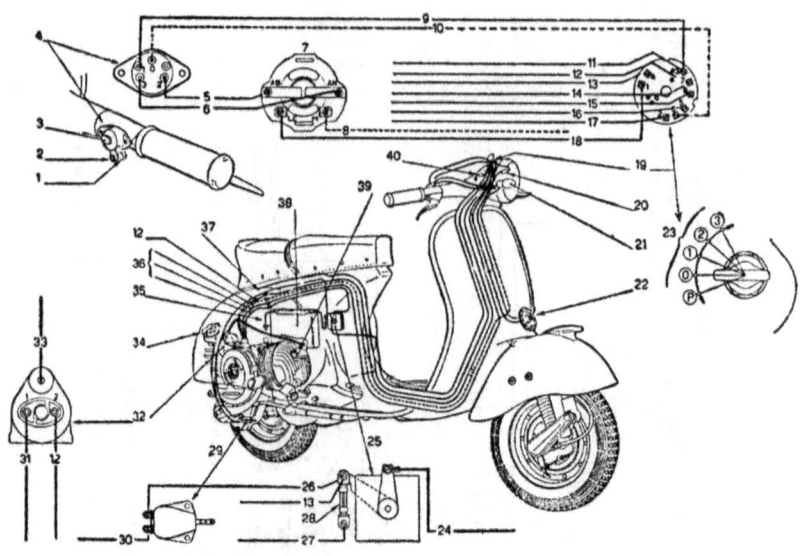
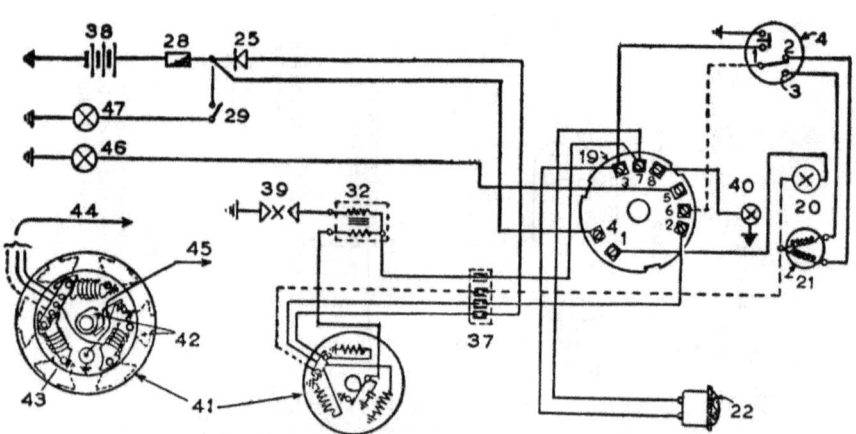

Fig. 36. Wiring on the G.S. Vespa Series VS 2

ELECTRICAL EQUIPMENT

Work on the rest of the electrical system amounts to little more than keeping a watchful eye on the various cables and checking them periodically for signs of damaged or perished insulation. All terminals should be examined for time to time, and cleaned if necessary. This includes the

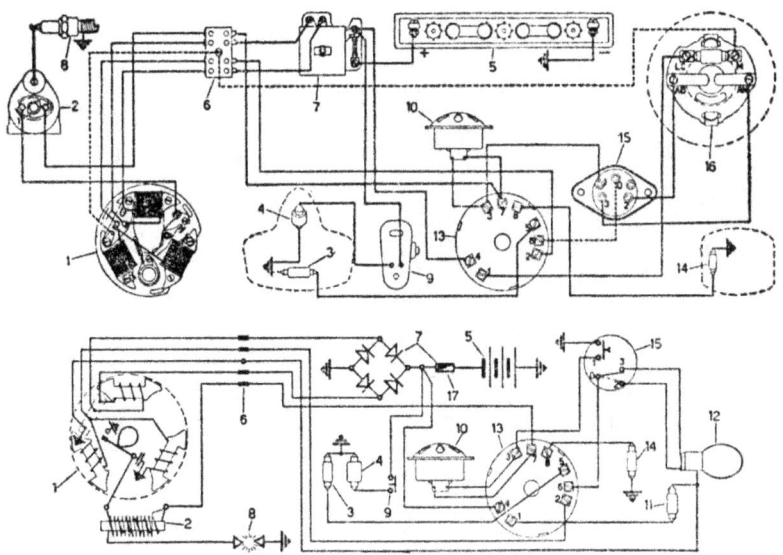

Fig. 37. The G.S. Vespa Series VS 4 Wiring layout

terminals in the handlebar switch, but in this case bear in mind the importance of disconnecting the battery leads first.

A trouble which sometimes occurs is blowing of the tail-bulb filament. This may be due not to an inherent electrical fault but to faulty riding technique. When the switch is operated to change from main to dipped beam, or vice-versa, the full electrical load can momentarily be applied to the tail-bulb, so drastically overloading the filament. To prevent this happening, it is best to ease the throttle closed slightly as the switch is operated, thus reducing the output momentarily.

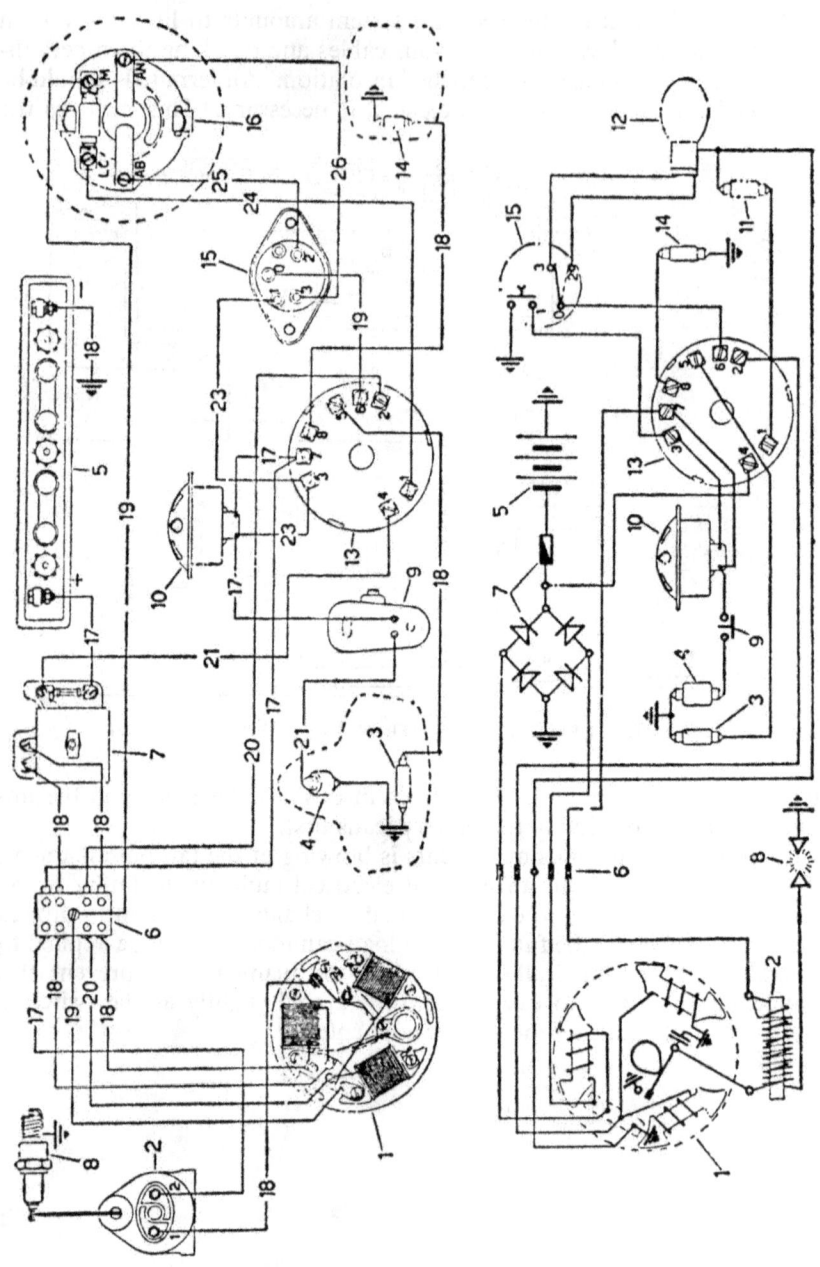

Fig. 38. Wiring of the G.S. Vespa VS 5 Series

9 Brakes, Tyres and Forks

THANKS to the constant development which the Vespa has undergone there is virtually nothing to do on the running gear of the machine, save to carry out the routine adjustments to the brake, throttle, clutch and gear control cables.

The rider's tendency subconsciously to accept the gradual deterioration in braking power as the linings wear has been mentioned earlier. So, too, has the need to carry out regular checks on the brake adjustment to combat this.

The brakes are both adjusted by varying the relative lengths of the inner and outer control cables. For the front brake, the screw-type adjuster, with lock-nut, is fitted on the brake plate itself. The rear brake adjuster is screwed into an abutment on the engine casing. In both cases, the lock-nut is loosened, and the adjuster is racked out until the brake is just binding and preventing the wheel from turning. At this point, the adjuster is released slightly and the wheel turned again. The adjustment is correct when the wheel can turn freely. So set, the brake will come on with the minimum of movement of its lever or pedal. The lock-nut is then tightened to hold the adjustment.

When no further adjustment remains the brake drums must be removed, and the brake-shoes eased from their pivots, against which they are spring loaded. Service exchange brake-shoes, which are ready lined, should be substituted for them. This is an altogether better method than attempting to reline the existing shoes. Before replacing the brake drums give the working surfaces a wipe with clean rag, and rid them of any dust which has accumulated. Drums which have become scored, or which have a noticeable degree of ovality—characterized by an "on-off-on" sensation when the brake is applied—must either be exchanged or taken to an engineering shop for truing and skimming.

When refitting or adjusting a front brake cable it is essential to see that a good loop of cable is left between the point at which the cable emerges from the base of the steering column and the operating lever on the hub. If there is insufficient slack at this point the action of the front suspension can cause the brake to be continually applied and released. So, before assuming a fault in the brake drum, ensure that the cable control itself is not the culprit.

It is important, too, to remember that the control levers and the brake cam spindles must be lubricated periodically. If this job is neglected

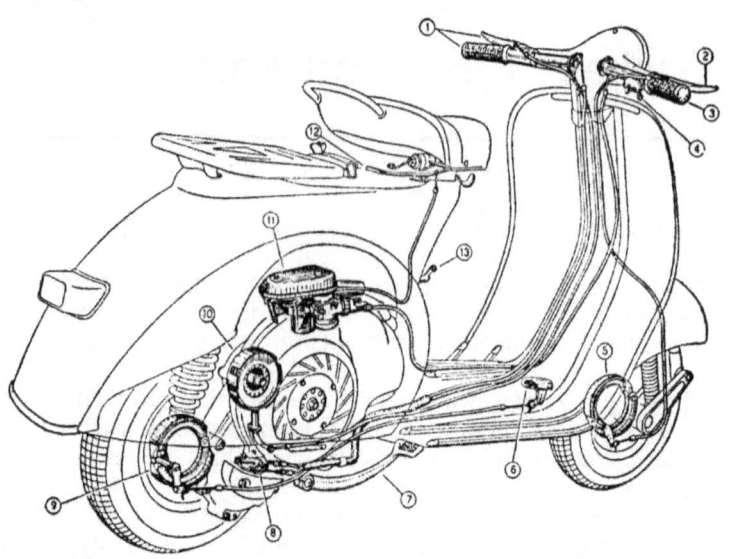

Fig. 39. How the Vespa Controls are Laid Out

1. Gear-change control and clutch lever
2. Front brake lever
3. Throttle
4. Lights and dip switch
5. Front brake shoes
6. Rear brake pedal
7. Kickstarter
8. Gear control plate
9. Rear brake shoes
10. Clutch
11. Carburettor
12. Choke control
13. Fuel tap

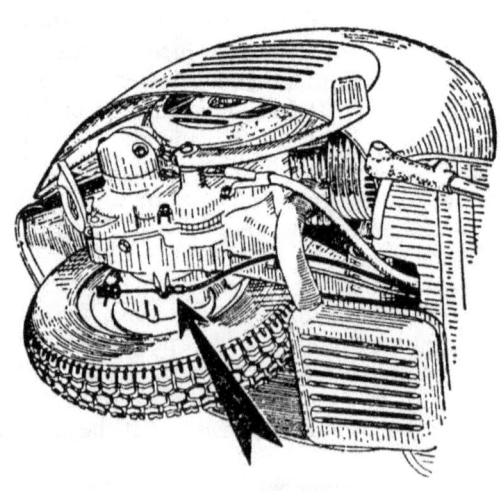

Fig. 40. The Position of the Rear Brake Adjuster 125 c.c. Model

BRAKES, TYRES AND FORKS 69

there is a danger that the parts may seize. Sticky operation of the brakes could almost certainly be attributed to insufficient attention to the lubrication of the cam pivots.

Breakage of the gear-change cables can often be traced to faulty assembly at the ferrule end. The twin cables are led through slots in the claws of the

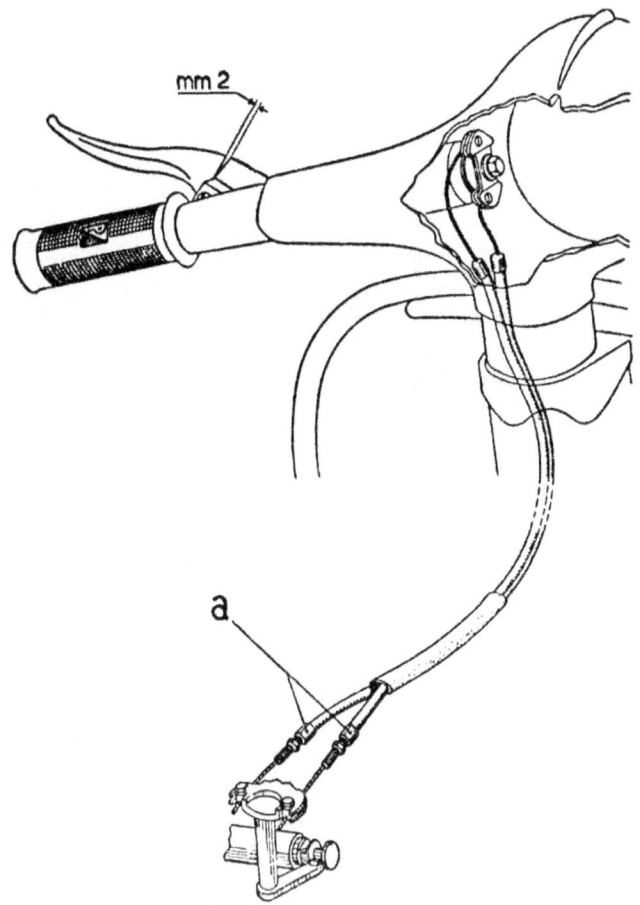

FIG. 41. How the Gear Control Cables Run
Adjustment in this case—the 150 c.c. model—is by means of twin cable adjusters, *a*. Clutch lever play is shown.

gear shifter, movement of the cables being transmitted to the claws by a ferrule screwed to each cable. Each ferrule has a hexagonal head, and if this should foul the edge of the claw the result is to allow the ferrule to turn with the claw, instead of revolving slightly. This results in bending of the cable and, eventually, in its failure through fatigue. Check this point when adjusting the gear control, and examine the edges of the claws for rough spots which would cause the ferrules to turn. If any are found, relieve them with a fine file.

A very fine clearance is specified for the adjustment of the clutch cable on the Vespa. As with most two-wheelers, this is given as free play at the

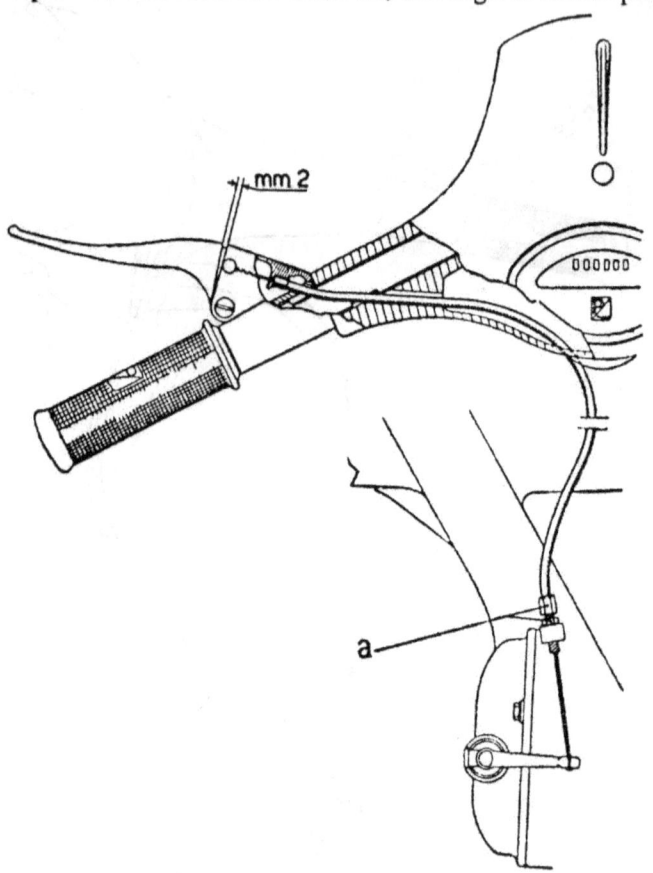

FIG. 42. CLUTCH CONTROL ADJUSTMENT

It is vital to maintain just the right play in the clutch control, using the adjuster (*a*) to obtain exactly 2-mm clearance at the lever.

handlebar end, and is measured between the edge of the lever and its abutment on the bars. If smooth gear-changing is to be obtained from the machine, only two millimetres of play is permissible. This calls for care in the use of the adjuster, since it is equally impermissible to have the adjuster set so that no play at all is present. This can lead to clutch slip, and to burning of the clutch plates.

The plates can also be damaged if the gearbox oil level is allowed to drop below the specified mark. The clutch and gearbox depend upon the same supply for their lubrication, but owing to the relatively high position of the clutch a low oil level will not provide it with the oil it needs. The cork inserts will therefore tend to dry out and, after that, to burn. When this happens considerable damage can be done.

Tyres, being non-mechanical, are often badly overlooked. They, however, require maintenance just as much as any other part of the machine. The pressure at which a tyre is run is all-important. If it is run soft, the sidewalls are subjected to bending loads, and continually flex. In time, they will crack and the tyre will be ruined. If, on the other hand, the

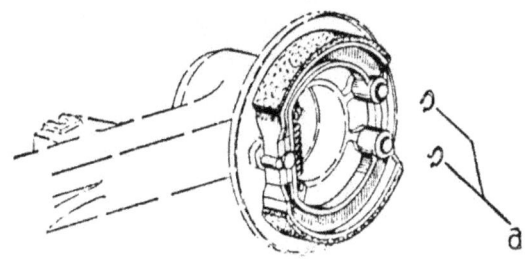

FIG. 43. ON THE G.S. THE BRAKE SHOES ARE SECURED BY TWO CIRCLIPS (*a*)

tyre is pumped up too hard there is a danger that sudden contact with a stone or a hole in the road will induce such a high momentary compression of the air in the tyre that the tube will burst. Hence the importance of maintaining the recommended pressures at all times, and of increasing the pressure in the rear tyre when a passenger is carried.

The tyre treads should be examined weekly, and any stones trapped in the treads should be carefully eased out. Many of the stones which a tyre picks up are sharp flints. Each time the tyre revolves the road surface presses on these flints and drives them a little farther into the rubber, rather like a nail being hammered through the tread. If left undisturbed, such stones can eventually pierce the tread and the casing and cause a blow-out of the tube. At the least, they reduce the life of the tyre, so the few minutes spent on this job are amply repaid by obtaining a better mileage from the tyre.

When inflating a tyre, it is also important to make sure that the dust cap is put back on its valve. The cap serves a dual purpose: it prevents dirt from entering and possibly jamming the valve, and it is itself an efficient seal which will keep the pressure in the tyre even if the valve leaks.

If the tyre is left undisturbed for a long period there is a chance that it may bond itself to the metal of the wheel rims. If this happens the tyre has to be sacrificed by being cut from the rim. Again, though there is no cure

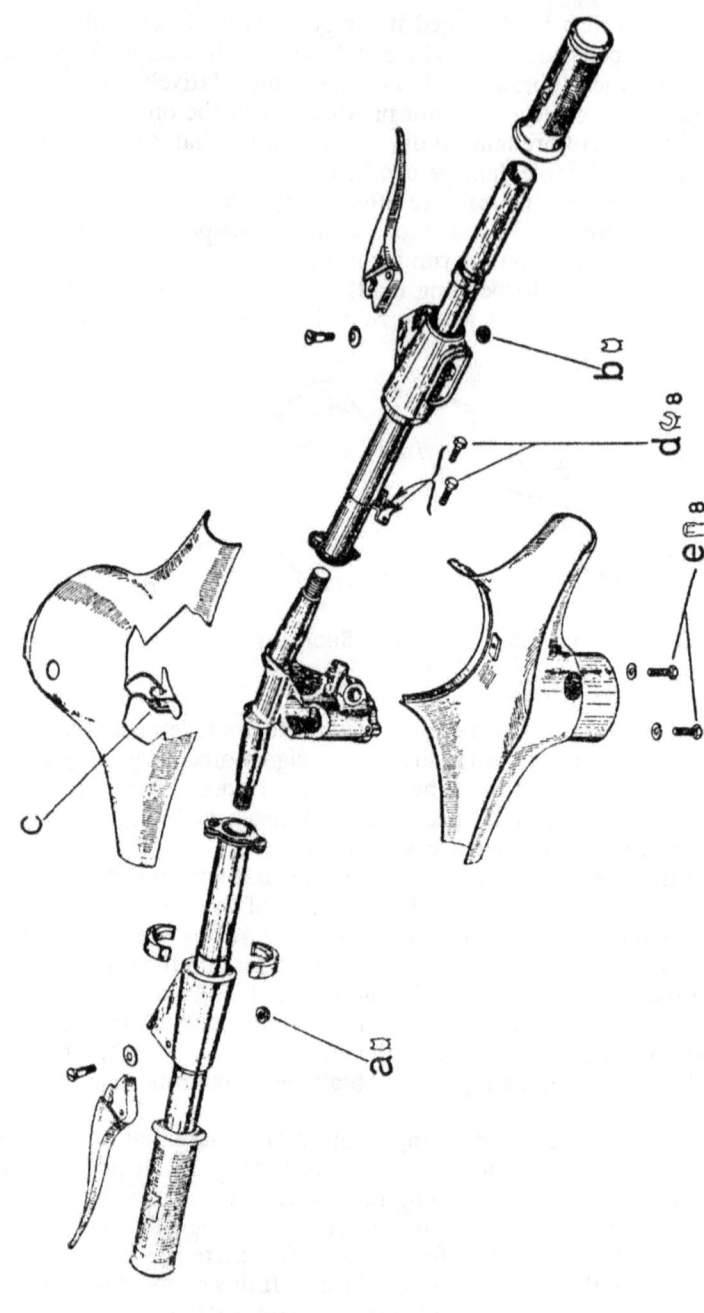

FIG. 44. THE LAYOUT OF THE 125 c.c. MACHINE'S HANDLEBAR ASSEMBLY
Note the specially-shaped screwdriver required for freeing the nuts (*a*) and (*b*).

whenever the fuel is switched on, and the engine, if it runs at all, constantly misfires and sounds "lumpy." Usually, it will not run, and the sparking plug, when removed, looks distinctly wet.

Only the float assembly can be responsible for overflooding. The float may have punctured, in which case it simply sinks to the bottom of the

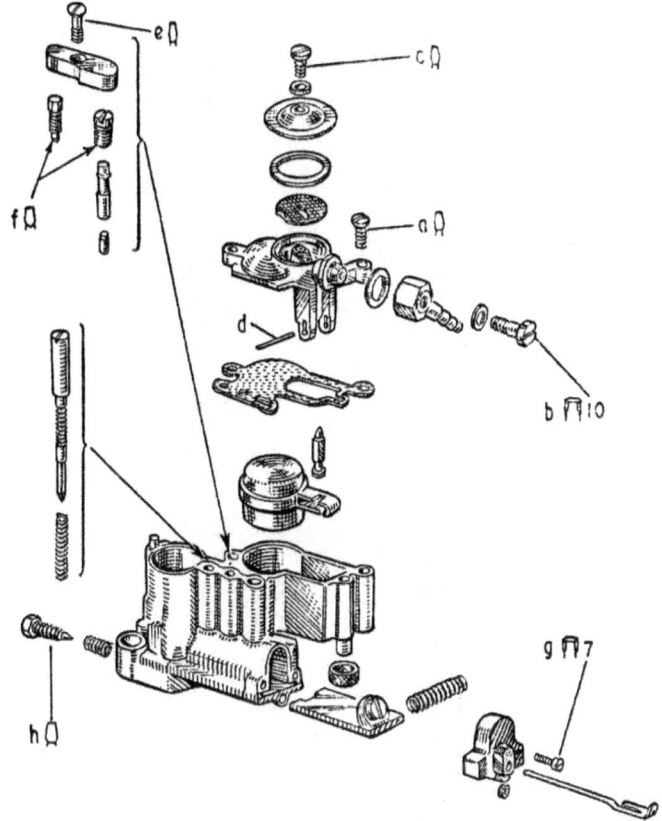

FIG. 46. THE UNUSUAL DELL' ORTO CARBURETTOR FITTED TO THE 150 c.c. STANDARD AND 150 c.c. SPORTIQUE MACHINES

Dismantle this in the order shown on the diagram, using the tools indicated.

chamber and leaves the valve wide open so that fuel simply pours in, or else a speck of grit has entered the valve seating and is preventing it from closing. In very rare cases the valve itself may have been damaged. This might possibly lead to a milder form of flooding which, though not severe enough to stop the engine, could cause it to misfire badly at lower speeds, when the fuel was not being fully used. In such cases, a very thorough check of the valve assembly must be made. Where flooding is severe, must obviously lie either in the filter or in the valve assembly. Examine them, clean them, and then reconnect the pipe and re-check.

Where no fuel flows from the pipe, however, again switch off and then detach the other end of the pipe from the fuel tap, since the blockage must obviously lie somewhere between the carburettor end of the pipe and the

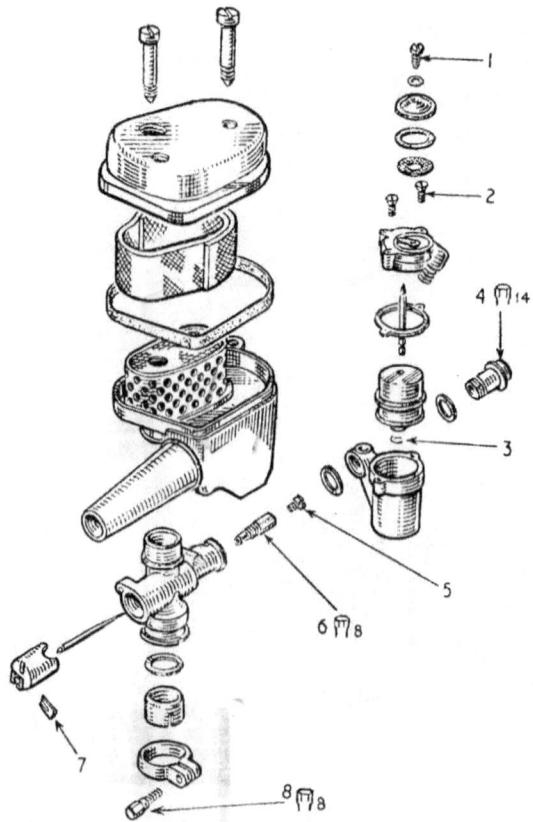

Fig. 45. Exploded View of the Carburettor Fitted to 125 c.c. Models

The figures show the order in which it must be dismantled

fuel tank—that is, in the pipe itself, in the tap, or in the tank. Once the pipe is off, switch on the fuel and check that it flows through the tank tap. If so, then the blockage must be in the pipe. If not, then the inference is that the tap itself is choked, and must be cleaned.

It is possible for the fuel system to be at fault by supplying too much fuel, as well as by supplying too little. Overflooding, as this form of trouble is called, is easily recognizable. Fuel drips from the carburettor

10 Fuel Systems and Carburettors

PROVIDED the correct petroil mixture is always used and that you are careful to obtain supplies from a clean pump, there is little work indeed which either need be done, or even can be done, on the fuel system. One rather puzzling fault which can occur, however, has a very simple cause and an even simpler solution.

Fuel starvation can be brought on if the vent hole in the tank filler cap becomes blocked. Since the tank is virtually sealed when the cap is locked down, save for this vent hole, blockage of the hole means that no air can enter. If air cannot enter, fuel cannot leave, since it is held by suction. In all cases of fuel starvation, first check that the vent hole is clear by poking through it with a piece of thin wire.

If this fails, disconnect the pipe at the carburettor end and turn the fuel on. Petroil should flow through. If not, you have isolated the point of blockage as being either in the fuel tap or the fuel pipe.

Where the carburettor has a tickler it is often sufficient to depress it for a matter of five seconds until the float chamber floods. If fuel drips from the carburettor when the tickler is held down it proves that the fault is not in the supply system. When you are doubtful about it, remove the top of the float chamber and examine the contents of the float chamber itself. Switch the tap off first, remove the top of the chamber, and then switch on again. Petroil should immediately flow through the valve. That eliminates the whole of the fuel line as far as the float chamber. Next, examine the fuel in the chamber. If it is dirty—especially if the bottom of the chamber contains sediment—it is an indication that the fault must lie in the instrument itself. Usually, it can be traced to a choked filter or to a blocked jet. Dismantling and examination will give the answer.

Let us assume, though, that no fuel is reaching the carburettor. Again, rectification depends primarily upon isolating the exact seat of the trouble, and in this case it is best to work backwards from the float chamber towards the tank.

Take off the float-chamber lid, and again switch on the petroil, working the needle valve assembly with your fingers to check that it opens and closes. Then, if no fuel comes through, switch off the petroil and detach the fuel pipe from the union on the float chamber. Switch the fuel on again to see if it is flowing through the pipe. If it does there should be quite a strong stream of fuel, not just a trickle, and if such a flow results the fault it is easy enough to prevent this happening. Periodically, remove the wheel, deflate the tyre, and release the bolts holding the split rim together. Detach the rims, and clean the bead seats thoroughly. Take out the tube, brush away any dirt which you find trapped in the case, and then liberally dust the tube and the tyre beads with french chalk before replacing them on the wheel rims.

For the rest, maintenance of the Vespa running gear entails nothing more complicated than keeping a watchful eye open for loose nuts and bolts; adhering to the greasing and general lubrication routine; and cleaning the paintwork and chromium plating.

remove the float and shake it. If it is punctured some fuel will be trapped inside, and you will be able to hear it swishing about. A damaged float *can* be soldered, but it is better to fit a new one and take no chances.

If the needle valve and float mechanism both pass muster, the final suspect must be the main jet. Remove this and blow through it, from the end opposite to the normal direction of travel of the fuel, to clear the

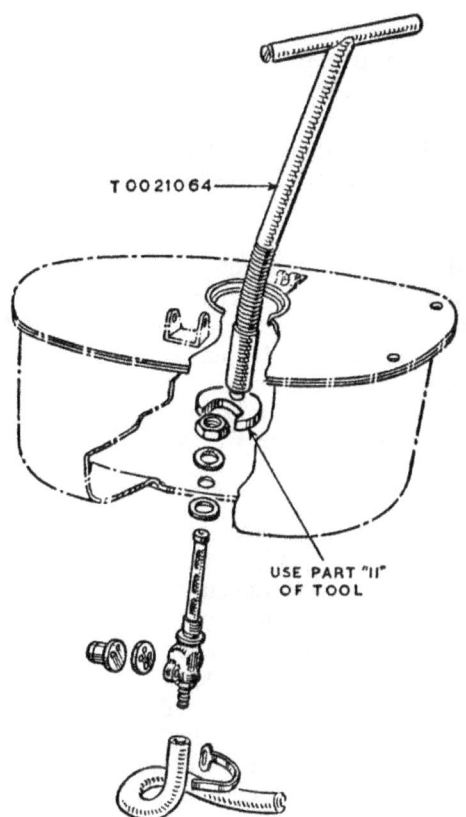

FIG. 47. A SPECIAL SPANNER IS NEEDED TO REMOVE THE FUEL TAP

fine metering hole. Never attempt to clear a main jet by poking it with wire, or a needle. The jet is designed to meter an almost microscopic amount of fuel, and it is made of very soft metal. Jabbing it with the harder metal used in wire or in needles is quite sufficient to enlarge the jet orifice and throw the carburation completely out. At the most, a stiff bristle could be used to clear a really badly blocked jet.

Always bear in mind that a carburettor is a relatively delicate scientific instrument, finely balanced internally to perform a very exacting job Scrupulous cleanliness and care must be exercised in stripping and cleaning

11 Drive and the Controls

IF a novice were asked to step into an aeroplane and fly it away with no other instruction than a cursory explanation of the controls he would refuse point-blank, yet the beginner who buys a scooter is often expected to find out for himself how to ride the machine. Quite frequently, he has to do his learning on some of the most crowded roads in Europe.

Of course a Vespa is relatively easy to handle, and is also an inherently safe machine, but the fact remains that teaching oneself is not the ideal way of learning the art of scooter riding.

In some parts of the country it is possible to enrol for a course of instruction under the R.A.C./A-C.U. Learner Training Scheme. Besides riding lessons, the course includes lectures which help the learner to understand his machine. Operated on a voluntary basis by A-C.U.-affiliated clubs, these courses are inexpensive and good. Details of them are available from the Manager, R.A.C. Motor-cycle Department, 85 Pall Mall, London, S.W.1.

Unfortunately, the Scheme is not operating in every area—road safety would be greatly enhanced if it were—so for some riders self-tuition still has to fill the gap. That being so it is essential not to form bad habits, for these subsequently become very difficult to break. The style which the learner-rider evolves at this formative stage of his novitiate will determine not only whether he becomes a safe and skilled rider, but also how much strain he imposes on his machine. Much wear and tear can be saved by riding habits alone, provided they are good ones.

As a first step in learning to ride, settle down in an armchair and learn exactly where all the controls are, and what they do. The Vespa layout is standardized for all models. On the right handlebar is a twist-grip. This controls the throttle. Twist it towards you and the throttle opens, so speeding up the engine. Twist it away from you and the throttle closes, slowing the engine. Also on the right bar is the lever controlling the front brake, one of the most important of controls.

Matching these, on the left bar, are a twist-grip which enables you to select the gears, and a clutch lever which permits the machine to be moved from rest by progressively engaging the clutch plates, as already described. The clutch lever moves up and down with the gear control.

On the footboard is the pedal controlling the rear brake. Mounted alongside the engine is the kickstarter, and on the bodywork you will find the fuel tap. The switchgear is fitted on the handlebar fairing.

DRIVING AND THE CONTROLS

Once you have memorized the position of each control, spend a quarter of an hour sitting on the machine and operating each of them in turn. Practise finding the various levers and the footbrake pedal instinctively, without having to look for them.

Next, practise starting the engine. Turn on the petrol and ignition, choke the engine if it is a cold day, open the throttle about an eighth of an inch, and operate the kickstarter. Make sure the machine is not in gear; then give a good swing with your leg—not so much a kick as a long, steady

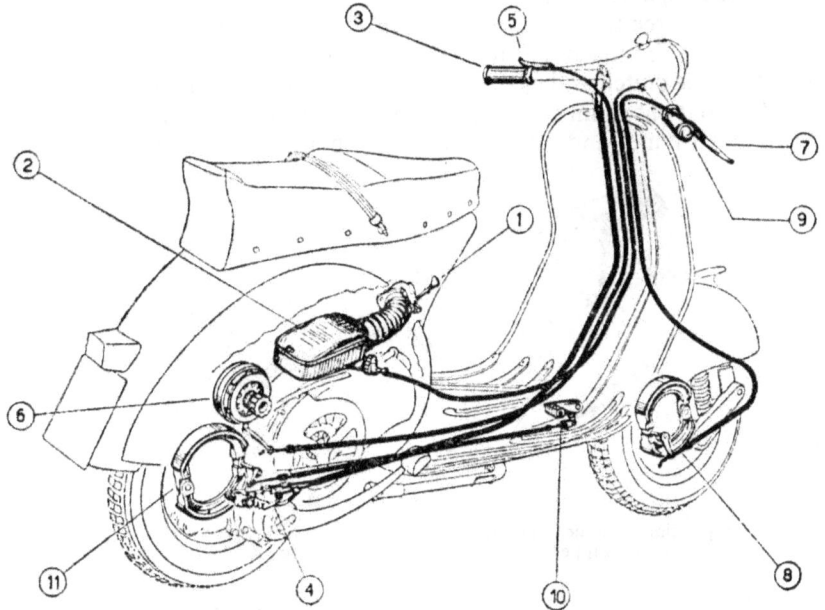

FIG. 48. HOW THE CONTROLS OF THE G.S. VESPA ARE DISPOSED

1. Choke rod
2. Carburettor
3. Gear-change twist-grip
4. Gear control plate
5. Clutch lever
6. Clutch
7. Front brake lever
8. Front brake shoes
9. Throttle
10. Rear brake pedal
11. Rear brake shoes

propelling movement of the foot. Keep the throttle opening steady, and the engine should fire. Keep it running and test the response of the engine to movement of the throttle control. Don't over-rev it, though.

Once the engine has been started the next obvious step is to go somewhere—but don't fall for that temptation at once. Instead, keep the engine running, push the machine off the stand, and straddle it. Withdraw the clutch by pulling the lever fully back to the handlebar, and turn the twist-grip to select first gear. Now try to master the art of moving away from a standstill. You have to learn to co-ordinate the movement of the fingers of your left hand with a gentle movement of your right which will open the throttle as the clutch takes up the drive.

So, keeping the throttle opening steady, begin to unfold your left hand from the knuckles so that the clutch lever is gradually released. As it reaches the point at which the clutch plates are beginning to take up the drive you feel the machine begin to edge forward. Stop your hand movement here momentarily, then pull out the clutch again and select neutral. This gives the clutch a moment or two to rest before you repeat the exercise again. Don't do it too often—it's not good for the clutch—just two or three times, to give yourself the feel of the thing.

Now take the machine on to the road, start the engine, engage gear, withdraw the clutch and again release the lever slowly. This time, though, don't whip it out again as it begins to bite. Instead, just stay the movement of your left hand, and open the throttle about a quarter of an inch with

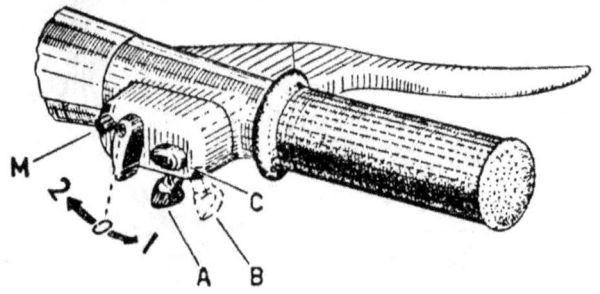

Fig. 49. The Switchgear on the 125 c.c. Model

In position 1 the head and tail lamps are on; in 2, the pilot lamp and tail lamp; in A the dipped beam; and in B the main beam. At O all lights are off.

your right. Immediately, the machine will start to move. Lift both feet on to the footboards, and release the clutch fully. You are now under way, controlling your speed with the throttle just as a cyclist with a fixed wheel controls his speed with the pedals. Practise varying the speed with the throttle as you ride along. Then close the throttle, apply the brakes, and withdraw the clutch. The machine will come to rest. You can then put the gear control into neutral, and release the clutch.

Continue practising take-offs and low-speed control until you are confident. Then you can take matters a stage further and learn how to change gear. Speed up to about 10 m.p.h. in bottom gear. Then simultaneously slam the throttle shut and whip out the clutch. Both movements *must* be co-ordinated. With the clutch out, turn the gear control to the second-gear position, and let the clutch out fast. Then open the throttle again. Repeat the procedure for changes into third gear, and into fourth for a four-speed model.

To change down again, withdraw the clutch and give a flick on the throttle; quarter of an inch open, then quickly closed again. As you blip the throttle, shift the gear control into the next-lowest gear position and immediately re-engage the clutch. Later on, you will be able to make clutchless changes; but not yet.

To make a turn, start with slow-speed turns at the end of your run. Slow down to walking pace in first gear, glance behind, and make sure the road is clear for at least 150 yards behind you and the same in front. Give the appropriate "turning right signal," lean the machine to the right, turning the bars slightly as you do so, and allow it to turn round until it is facing in the opposite direction. You may have to open the throttle a little to help it. Try to keep your feet up; trailing feet only unbalance you and could get painfully trapped by the footboard if you *did* happen to drop the machine.

More especially if their previous experience has been confined to riding a pedal cycle, most learners make the mistake of using only the rear brake and ignoring the front one when stopping. This is almost exactly the opposite of the correct technique, since the front brake is the more powerful and the one less likely to provoke a skid. Consequently, it should always be given a "lead" over the rear brake. The reason is simple. Whenever the brakes are applied a transference of weight occurs from the rear to the front of the machine, and this holds the front wheel hard to the road. If the rear brake alone is applied the transfer is in the same direction, so the rear wheel adhesion is reduced, and braking power with it.

Practise braking, first of all, with gentle applications of the front brake only; then with the front brake applied slightly first, followed by the rear brake. Don't jam the brakes on; apply each gently at first, increasing the pressure steadily as the machine slows. Just before it halts withdraw the clutch, and the result should be a good straight-line stop. Later on, you will learn to use the throttle and the gearbox to aid deceleration and for restricting the machine's speed when descending hills.

Like a bicycle, a scooter is steered by being leaned to one side or the other, but unlike a bicycle its handlebars are never perceptibly turned, save at very low speeds. When a two-wheeler is made to turn, the previously balanced forces which were maintaining its equilibrium are upset by the arrival of another force—centrifugal force—which tends to pull it across the road away from the centre of the turn.

If the turn was made with the machine upright the rider would either have to let it skid outwards, or else incline his own weight to balance this upsetting force. Neither solution is easy; so instead the machine is leaned into the turn. This has two effects. Owing to the castor action, it causes the front wheel to point into the direction of turn; and it also moves the centre of gravity of the machine to one side. If the machine happened to be stationary it would topple over towards the side to which it had been leaned. This, of course, is opposite to the side to which centrifugal force is trying to drag it. Thus, leaning the machine over sets up a second out-of-balance force to oppose the first. The two neutralize each other, and the machine simply turns.

Much of the work of cornering is done before the corner is reached. The object is, quite simply, to arrive at the corner at the right speed, in the right gear, and at the right point on the road. All braking and slowing must be done before the corner is reached, so that when you get there all you have to do is to choose the moment when you can *just* see through the bend, bank the machine over, and gently open the throttle to accelerate through it. Generally speaking, left-hand bends should be approached from just left of the centre-line of the road; right-handers from a foot or so from the left-hand kerb. But in each case the governing factor must be the other traffic on the road; a slow-moving scooter should not be placed out in the centre of a road with fast cars streaming up at high speeds behind it.

SIDECAR WORK

Vespas are great favourites for sidecar work, but driving a "chair" is something quite distinct from solo riding. One of the greatest mistakes made by newcomers to sidecars is to oversteer. Sidecar machines have very sensitive steering—equivalent to direct steering on a car—and consequently a minute amount of handlebar movement is sufficient to make them turn. If the bars are visibly deflected from their central position the resulting turn will be very sharp indeed. For all normal work the bars are not so much turned as pressed, very gently, with the palm of the appropriate hand.

No vehicle on the road has greater stability than the sidecar outfit, but none will lift one wheel so easily, either, if it is mishandled. The reasons behind this should be fully understood.

When a sidecar is turned to the left, centrifugal force tries to pull it to the right, just as with the solo. Since the scooter's wheels resist this pull, the centrifugal force has the effect of lightening the load on the sidecar. It tries, in fact, to pull the sidecar up, pivoting about the wheels of the scooter. If a left-hand corner is taken too fast, this upsetting force can be of sufficient magnitude to lift the sidecar wheel right off the ground.

On a right-hand bend the same thing happens, only in reverse. This time it is the scooter which loses adhesion. The forces are trying to pull it over the sidecar, and if they are strong enough they can in fact cause the rear wheel to lift. The machine then pivots on a base-line formed by the scooter's front wheel and the sidecar wheel. If the forces are strong enough, in fact, the machine can even somersault.

Drastic though this sounds, prevention is simple. The solo rider would fare no better, save that he can incline his machine to oppose these forces. The sidecar driver cannot, so instead he uses acceleration and deceleration to offset centrifugal force.

On a left-hand bend, the machine is accelerated. This produces a force

DRIVING AND THE CONTROLS

acting inwards towards the centre of the turn, balancing the outwards-acting centrifugal force. On a right-hand bend, however, the throttle is closed and the brakes applied very gently. This might seem illogical at first sight, but since the effect is to slow the scooter wheels but to leave the free-running sidecar wheel unbraked, the effect is exactly the same as if the scooter had run on at the same speed and the sidecar wheel had been accelerated.

Another peculiarity of the sidecar outfit is its braking. If the bars were left pointing dead ahead and the brakes were applied, the machine would swing to the right. This is, of course, a result of the sidecar wheel being unbraked. Though the scooter wheels slowed, the sidecar wheel would run on and turn the sidecar round the machine. When braking, therefore, it is essential to apply a gentle left pressure to the bars to hold the machine straight.

Under slippery conditions a sidecar comes into its own, the free-rolling sidecar wheel positively resisting attempts to deflect it out of its course. As soon as a slide develops it tries to push the sidecar wheel sideways. This the wheel will not stand; it tries immediately to return to its normal place, and thus automatically corrects the skid.

Though extremely safe under such conditions, a sidecar outfit must be maintained in correct alignment if it is not to be tiring to drive. If it is hard to steer it is misaligned, as a rule, and the settings must be professionally adjusted to bring them within the limits specified by the manufacturer.

APPENDIX A – LUBRICATION CHARTS

ALL MODELS 125 c.c. and CLUBMAN

Part to be lubricated		Lubrication				
Every 2,500	Every 5,000	**Shell*	**B.P.*	*Esso*	*Wakefield*	*Mobil*
Gearbox topping-up	Gearbox change oil	Shell 2T Two-Stroke Oil or Shell X-100 30	Energol Two-Stroke Oil or Energol S.A.E. 30	Esso Extra Motor Oil 20W/30	Castrol XL	Mobiloil A
Front suspension Felt pad on fly-wheel cam Joints on brake control Speedo flexible drive	Control cables Gear-change quadrant	Retinax A	Energrease L.2	Esso Multi-Purpose Grease H	Castrolease L.M.	Mobilgrease M.P
Engine at each refuelling		Shell 2T Two-Stroke Oil in ratio of 5% or $\frac{1}{2}$ pint to $1\frac{1}{4}$ gal petrol	Energol Two-Stroke Oil in ratio of 5% or $\frac{1}{2}$ pint to $1\frac{1}{4}$ gal petrol	Essolube 30 in ratio of 5% or $\frac{1}{2}$ pint to $1\frac{1}{4}$ gal petrol. Esso Two-StrokeMotorOil in ratio of $\frac{3}{4}$ pint to $1\frac{1}{4}$ gal petrol	Castrol XL in ratio of 5% or $\frac{1}{2}$ pint to $1\frac{1}{4}$ gal petrol. Castrol Two-Stroke Oil in ratio of $\frac{3}{4}$ pint to $1\frac{1}{4}$ gal petrol	Mobiloil A in ratio of 5% or $\frac{1}{2}$ pint to $1\frac{1}{4}$ gal petrol or Mobil-Mix in ratio of $\frac{3}{4}$ pint to $1\frac{1}{4}$ gal petrol

* Marketed also by National Benzole Co. Ltd., by arrangement with Shell-Mex & B.P. Ltd.

APPROVED PETROL/OIL MIXTURE

Make	Description
Shell	2T Two-Stroke Mixture
B.P.	B.P.-Zoom
National Benzole Co. Ltd.	Hi-Fli

150 c.c. ROTARY VALVE MODELS

Part to be lubricated			Lubrication				
After first 600 miles	Every 2,500 miles	Every 5,000 miles	*Shell	*B.P.	Esso	Wakefield	Mobil
Gearbox change oil	Gearbox topping-up	Gearbox change oil	Shell 2T Two-Stroke Oil or Shell X-100 30	Energol Two-Stroke Oil or Energol S.A.E. 30	Esso Extra Motor Oil 20W/30	Castrol XL	Mobiloil A
	Front suspension Felt pad on flywheel cam Joints on brake control Speedo flexible drive	Control cables Gear-change quadrant	Retinax A	Energrease L.2	Esso Multi-Purpose Grease H	Castrolease L.M.	Mobilgrease M.P.
	Engine at each refuelling		Shell 2T Two-Stroke Oil in ratio of 2% or ¼ pint to 1½ gal petrol	Energol Two-Stroke Oil in ratio of 2% or ¼ pint to 1½ gal petrol	Essolube 30 in ratio of 2% or ¼ pint to 1½ gal petrol. Esso Two-StrokeMotorOil in ratio of ¼ pint to 1 gal petrol	Castrol XL in ratio of 2% or ¼ pint to 1½ gal petrol. Castrol Two-Stroke Oil in ratio of ¼ pint 1 gal petrol	Mobiloil A in ratio of 2% or ¼ pint to 1½ gal petrol. Mobil-Mix in ratio of ¼ pint to 1 gal petrol

* Marketed also by National Benzole Co. Ltd., by arrangement with Shell-Mex & B.P. Ltd.

Approved Petrol/Oil Mixture

Make	Description	
Shell	2T Two-Stroke Mixture	To be used with equal parts of neat petrol.
B.P.	B.P.-Zoom	
National Benzole Co. Ltd.	Hi-Fli	

ALL 150 c.c. G.S. MODELS

Part to be lubricated		Lubrication				
		*Shell	*B.P.	Esso	Wakefield	Mobil
Every 2,500	Every 5,000					
	Gearbox change oil	Shell 2T Two-Stroke Oil or Shell X-100 30	Energol Two-Stroke Oil or Energol S.A.E. 30	Esso Extra Motor Oil 20W/30	Castrol XL	Mobiloil A
Gearbox topping-up						
Front suspension Felt pad on fly-wheel cam Joints on brake control Speedo flexible drive	Control cables Gear-change quadrant	Retinax A	Energrease L.2	Esso Multi-Purpose Grease H	Castrolease L.M.	Mobilgrease M.P.
Engine at each refuelling		Shell 2T Two-Stroke Oil in ratio of 6% or ½ pint to 1 gal petrol	Energol Two-Stroke Oil in ratio of 6% or ½ pint to 1 gal petrol	Essolube 30 in ratio of 6% or ½ pint to 1 gal petrol. Esso Two-StrokeMotorOil in ratio of ¾ pint to 1 gal petrol	Castrol XL in ratio of 6% or ½ pint to 1 gal petrol. Castrol Two-Stroke Oil in ratio of ¾ pint to 1 gal petrol	Mobiloil A in ratio of 6% or ½ pint to 1 gal petrol. Mobil-Mix in ratio of ¾-pint to 1 gal petrol

* Marketed also by National Benzole Co. Ltd., by arrangement with Shell-Mex & B.P. Ltd.

APPENDIX B
PLUG RECOMMENDATIONS, ALL MODELS

	K.L.G.		A.C.		LODGE		CHAMPION	
	Plug	Gap	Plug	Gap	Plug	Gap	Plug	Gap
All 125 c.c.	F.70	0·023 0·026	45 F	0·022	H.N.	0·022 0·026	L.86	0·020
Clubman	F.75	0·023 0·026	42 F	0·022	H.N.	0·022 0·026	L.86	0·020
New 150 c.c.	F.75	0·023 0·026	42 F	0·022	2 H.N.	0·022 0·026	L.81	0·025
150 c.c. model Prefixed "S"	F.70	0·023 0·026	45 F	0·022	H.N.	0·022 0·026	L.86	0·020
All 150 c.c. G.S.	F.E.80	0·023	44XL	0·022	2 H.L.N.	0·023	N.84	0·020

APPENDIX C
TYRE PRESSURE CHART (lb/sq in.) ALL MODELS

MODEL		DUNLOP			PIRELLI		
		Front	Rear	Sidecar	Front	Rear	Sidecar
All 125 c.c.	Solo	16	20	—	16	22	—
	Pillion	16	32	—	16	32	—
	Sidecar	16	24	16	18	24	16
All 150 c.c. models excluding G.S.	Solo	16	20	—	16	22	—
	Pillion	16	32	—	16	32	—
	Sidecar	16	24	16	18	24	16
All 150 c.c. G.S.	Solo	16	20	—	16	22	—
	Pillion	16	32	—	16	32	—

APPENDIX D
CARBURETTOR DATA

152/L2 Model	150 c.c. Rotary Valve Models	150 c.c. G.S. Model
Dell' Orto type UA 16 S1 *Fitted to Machines 0291—* *1099271* Main Jet 72 Pilot Jet 38 Jet Needle 2nd notch from top	*Dell' Orto type S.I. 20/17B.* Main Jet 100 Pilot Jet 42	*Dell' Orto type UB 23 53* Main Jet 105 Pilot Jet 45 Jet Needle centre notch
Mixture Screw adjustment 1-1½ turns out from "in" position	*Mixture Screw adjustment* 1-1½ turns out from "in" position	*Mixture Screw adjustment* 1-1½ turns out from "in" position
Throttle Slide adjustment By rotating knurled screw situated on mixing chamber cover	*Throttle Slide adjustment* By rotation of slotted screw situated in lid of air cleaner	*Throttle Slide adjustment* By rotation of screw set diagonally in carburettor body
Amal type 503/1 *Fitted to Machines from 1099272 onwards* Main Jet 70 Pilot Jet 20 Jet Needle variable according to engine requirement		
Mixture Screw adjustment 1-1½ turns out from "in" position.		
Throttle Slide adjustment By rotating knurled screw situated on mixing chamber cover		

Index

AIR filter, 9, 11, 13
Amal carburettor, 89

BATTERY, 30, 58-9
Big end, 36
Brake—
  adjustment, 67, 68
  removal, 49, 67, 71
Brakes, general, 2, 18, 19, 67, 78, 81, 83
Bulbs, see Electrical circuits

CABLES, 18, 19
Carburettor, 10, 12, 13, 74-7, 89. See also Amal and Dell' Orto
Clutch, 41-3, 49, 50, 52, 80
  adjustments, 70
Compression ratio, 6
Connecting rod, 4, 5
Contact breaker, 29, 56
Controls, 68, 70, 78, 80
Cornering, 81-3
Crankcase, 7, 8, 10, 42, 46, 52
Crankpin, 4, 5
Crankshaft, 4, 5
Cylinder, 4, 37
Cylinder head, 4, 36

DAILY maintenance, 24
Decarbonizing, 33-6
Dell' Orto carburettor, 76, 89

ELECTRICAL circuits, 30, 31, 57
Engine—
  overhaul, 32, 33, 40, 47, 48, 50-1, 58
  principles, 4-9
  types, 4-7
Exhaust system, 34

FAULT tracing, 27
Flywheel magneto, 40-1, 45, 47, 56-7
Front forks, 18
Fuel, 5, 10
Fuel tank, 27
Fuel troubles, 27

GEARBOX, 43, 52
Gearbox adjuster, 23, 69
Gear changing, 80
Gudgeon pin, 35-7

HANDLEBAR controls, 78
Handlebars, 72, 78
Headlamp, see Electrical circuits
Hydraulic dampers, 18

IGNITION—
  coil, 14-16
  faults, 28, 30
  leads, 28
  principles, 13-16
  timing, 15, 46

JETS, 10-13. See also Carburettor

KICK STARTER, 44-5, 78

LIGHTING, see Electrical circuits
Lubrication, 84-6

MAINTENANCE—
  daily, 24-5
  weekly, 25
  routine, 3, 23-6

OILS, etc., 26

PETROL, 10, 27
Petrol filters, 27, 74, 77
Petrol tap, 27, 77
Piston, 4-8, 34, 37
Piston rings, 29, 38-9

ROTARY valves, 8, 11, 47

SIDECARS, 82-3
Silencer, 35-6
Sparking plugs, 3, 28, 36, 56, 87
Specifications, 1
Steering head, 18
Suspension systems, 18
Switches, 80

TIMING—
 ignition, 46–7
 ports, 7
Tools, 2, 20–2, 46, 48, 50, 53. 55
Transmission, 16, 17

Twist grips, 78-9
Tyre pressures, 88
Tyres, 71, 73

WIRING diagrams, 57-66

ARE YOU:
INTERESTED IN EUROPEAN, IMPORT & EXOTIC AUTOMOBILES?

DO YOU:
DO YOUR OWN MAINTENANCE?

If you answered yes to either of these questions, then you should check out our automobile books and manuals. We have included a sample listing of some of our featured marques. However, for complete details and the most up-to-date information, please visit our website.

——— www.VelocePress.com ———

The fastest growing specialist USA publisher of niche market automotive books and manuals.

All VelocePress titles are available through your local independent bookseller, Amazon.com or direct from VelocePress. Wholesale customers may also purchase direct or from the Ingram Book Group.

AUTOBOOKS WORKSHOP MANUALS

ALFA ROMEO GIULIA 1300, 1600, 1750, 2000 1962-1978 WSM
AUSTIN HEALEY SPRITE, MG MIDGET 1958-1980 WSM
BMW 1600 1966-1973 WSM
BMW 2000 & 2002 1966-1976 WSM
BMW 2500, 2800, 3.0 & 3.3 1968-1977 WSM
BMW 316, 320, 320i 1975-1977 WSM
BMW 518, 520, 520i 1973-1981 WSM
FIAT 1100, 1100D, 1100R & 1200 1957-1969 WSM
FIAT 124 1966-1974 WSM
FIAT 124 SPORT 1966-1975 WSM
FIAT 125 & 125 SPECIAL 1967-1973 WSM
FIAT 126, 126L, 126 DV, 126/650 & 126/650 DV 1972-1982 WSM
FIAT 127 SALOON, SPECIAL & SPORT, 900, 1050 1971-1981 WSM
FIAT 128 1969-1982 WSM
FIAT 1300, 1500 1961-1967 WSM
FIAT 131 MIRAFIORI 1975-1982 WSM
FIAT 132 1972-1982 WSM
FIAT 500 1957-1973 WSM
FIAT 600, 600D & MULTIPLA 1955-1969 WSM
FIAT 850 1964-1972 WSM
JAGUAR E-TYPE 1961-1972 WSM
JAGUAR MK 1, 2 1955-1969 WSM
JAGUAR S TYPE, 420 1963-1968 WSM
JAGUAR XK 120, 140, 150 MK 7, 8, 9 1948-1961 WSM
LAND ROVER 1, 2 1948-1961 WSM
MERCEDES-BENZ 190 1959-1968 WSM
MERCEDES-BENZ 220/8 1968-1972 WSM
MERCEDES-BENZ 220B 1959-1965 WSM
MERCEDES-BENZ 230 1963-1968 WSM
MERCEDES-BENZ 250 1968-1972 WSM
MERCEDES-BENZ 280 1968-1972 WSM
MG MIDGET TA-TF 1936-1955 WSM
MINI 1959-1980 WSM
MORRIS MINOR 1952-1971 WSM
PEUGEOT 404 1960-1975 WSM
PORSCHE 911 1964-1973 WSM
PORSCHE 911 1970-1977 WSM
RENAULT 16 1965-1979 WSM
RENAULT 8, 10, 1100 1962-1971 WSM
ROVER 3500, 3500S 1968-1976 WSM
SUNBEAM RAPIER, ALPINE 1955-1965 WSM
TRIUMPH SPITFIRE, GT6, VITESSE 1962-1968 WSM
TRIUMPH TR2, TR3, TR3A 1952-1962 WSM
TRIUMPH TR4, TR4A 1961-1967 WSM
VOLKSWAGEN BEETLE 1968-1977 WSM

BROOKLANDS BOOKS & ROAD TEST PORTFOLIOS (RTP)

AC CARS 1904-2009
ALFA ROMEO 1920-1933 ROAD TEST PORTFOLIO
ALFA ROMEO 1934-1940 ROAD TEST PORTFOLIO
BRABHAM RALT HONDA THE RON TAURANAC STORY
BUGATTI TYPE 10 TO TYPE 40 ROAD TEST PORTFOLIO
BUGATTI TYPE 10 TO TYPE 251 ROAD TEST PORTFOLIO
BUGATTI TYPE 41 TO TYPE 55 ROAD TEST PORTFOLIO
BUGATTI TYPE 57 TO TYPE 251 ROAD TEST PORTFOLIO
DELAHAYE ROAD TEST PORTFOLIO
FERRARI ROAD CARS 1946-1956 ROAD TEST PORTFOLIO
FIAT 500 1936-1972 ROAD TEST PORTFOLIO
FIAT DINO ROAD TEST PORTFOLIO
HISPANO SUIZA ROAD TEST PORTFOLIO
HONDA ST1100/ST1300 PAN EUROPEAN 1990-2002 RTP
JAGUAR MK1 & MK2 ROAD TEST PORTFOLIO
LOTUS CORTINA ROAD TEST PORTFOLIO
MV AGUSTA F4 750 & 1000 1997-2007 ROAD TEST PORTFOLIO
TATRA CARS ROAD TEST PORTFOLIO

VELOCEPRESS AUTOMOBILE BOOKS & MANUALS

ABARTH BUYERS GUIDE
AUSTIN-HEALEY 6-CYLINDER WSM
BMW 600 LIMOUSINE FACTORY WSM
BMW 600 LIMOUSINE OWNERS HAND BOOK & SERVICE MANUAL
BMW ISETTA FACTORY WSM
BOOK OF THE CARRERA PANAMERICANA - MEXICAN ROAD RACE
COMPLETE CATALOG OF JAPANESE MOTOR VEHICLES
DIALED IN - THE JAN OPPERMAN STORY
FERRARI 250/GT SERVICE AND MAINTENANCE
FERRARI 308 SERIES BUYER'S AND OWNER'S GUIDE
FERRARI BERLINETTA LUSSO
FERRARI BROCHURES AND SALES LITERATURE 1946-1967
FERRARI BROCHURES AND SALES LITERATURE 1968-1989
FERRARI GUIDE TO PERFORMANCE
FERRARI OPP, MAINTENANCE & SERVICE H/BOOKS 1948-1963
FERRARI OWNER'S HANDBOOK
FERRARI SERIAL NUMBERS PART I - ODD NUMBERS TO 21399
FERRARI SERIAL NUMBERS PART II - EVEN NUMBERS TO 1050
FERRARI SPYDER CALIFORNIA
FERRARI TUNING TIPS & MAINTENANCE TECHNIQUES
HENRY'S FABULOUS MODEL "A" FORD
HOW TO BUILD A FIBERGLASS CAR
HOW TO BUILD A RACING CAR
HOW TO RESTORE THE MODEL 'A' FORD
IF HEMINGWAY HAD WRITTEN A RACING NOVEL
JAGUAR E-TYPE 3.8 & 4.2 WSM
LE MANS 24 (THE BOOK THAT THE FILM WAS BASED ON)
MASERATI BROCHURES AND SALES LITERATURE
MASERATI OWNER'S HANDBOOK
METROPOLITAN FACTORY WSM
MGA & MGB OWNERS HANDBOOK & WSM
OBERT'S FIAT GUIDE
PERFORMANCE TUNING THE SUNBEAM TIGER
PORSCHE 356 1948-1965 WSM
PORSCHE 912 WSM
SOUPING THE VOLKSWAGEN
TRIUMPH TR2, TR3, TR4 1953-1965 WSM
VEDA ORR'S NEW REVISED HOT ROD PICTORIAL
VOLKSWAGEN TRANSPORTER, TRUCKS, STATION WAGONS WSM
VOLVO 1944-1968 ALL MODELS WSM

VELOCEPRESS MOTORCYCLE BOOKS & MANUALS

AJS SINGLES 1955-65 350cc & 500cc (BOOK OF)
ARIEL 1939-1960 4 STROKE SINGLES (BOOK OF)
ARIEL LEADER & ARROW 1958-1964 (BOOK OF)
ARIEL MOTORCYCLES 1933-1951 WSM
ARIEL PREWAR MODELS 1932-1939 (BOOK OF)
BMW M/CYCLES R26 R27 (1956-1967) FACTORY WSM
BMW M/CYCLES R50 R50S R60 R69S (1955-1969) FACTORY WSM
BSA BANTAM (BOOK OF)
BSA ALL FOUR-STROKE SINGLES & V-TWINS 1936-1952 (BOOK OF)
BSA OHV & SV SINGLES - 250cc 1954-1970 (BOOK OF)
BSA OHV & SV SINGLES 1945-54 250-600cc (BOOK OF)
BSA OHV SINGLES 350 & 500cc 1955-1967 (BOOK OF)
BSA PRE-WAR MODELS TO 1939 (BOOK OF)
BSA TWINS 1948-1962 (BOOK OF)
BSA TWINS 1962-1969 (SECOND BOOK OF)
CATALOG OF BRITISH MOTORCYCLES (1951 MODELS)
DOUGLAS PRE-WAR ALL MODELS 1929-1939 (BOOK OF)
DOUGLAS POST-WAR ALL MODELS 1948-1957 FACTORY WSM
DUCATI 160cc, 250cc & 350cc OHC MODELS FACTORY WSM
HONDA 50 ALL MODELS UP TO 1970 INC MONKEY & TRAIL (BOOK OF)
HONDA 90 ALL MODELS UP TO 1966 (BOOK OF)
HONDA MOTORCYCLES 125-150 TWINS C/CS/CB/CA WSM
HONDA MOTORCYCLES 250-305 TWINS C/CS/CB WSM
HONDA MOTORCYCLES C100 SUPER CUB WSM
HONDA MOTORCYCLES C110 SPORT CUB 1962-1969 WSM
HONDA TWINS & SINGLES 50cc TO 305cc 1960-1966 (BOOK OF)
HONDA TWINS ALL MODELS 125cc THRU 450cc UP TO 1968 (BOOK OF)
INDIAN PONYBIKE, BOY RACER & PAPOOSE ILL PARTS LIST & SALES LIT
LAMBRETTA ALL 125 & 150cc MODELS 1947-1957 (BOOK OF)
LAMBRETTA LI & TV MODELS 1957-1970 (SECOND BOOK OF)
MATCHLESS 350 & 500cc SINGLES 1945-1956 (BOOK OF)
MATCHLESS 350 & 500cc SINGLES 1955-1966 (BOOK OF)
NORTON 1938-1956 (BOOK OF)
NORTON DOMINATOR TWINS 1955-1965 (BOOK OF)
NORTON MODELS 19, 50 & ES2 1955-1963 (BOOK OF)
NORTON MOTORCYCLES 1957-1970 FACTORY WSM
NORTON PREWAR MODELS 1932-1939 (BOOK OF)
ROYAL ENFIELD SINGLES & V TWINS 1937-1953 (BOOK OF)
ROYAL ENFIELD 736cc INTERCEPTOR FACTORY WSM
ROYAL ENFIELD 250cc & 350cc SINGLES 1958-1966 (SECOND BOOK OF)
SUZUKI 50cc & 80cc UP TO 1966 (BOOK OF)
SUZUKI T10 1963-1967 FACTORY WSM
SUZUKI T20 & T200 1965-1969 FACTORY WSM
TRIUMPH PRE-WAR MOTORCYCLE 1935-1939 (BOOK OF)
TRIUMPH MOTORCYCLES 1937-1951 WSM
TRIUMPH MOTORCYCLES 1945-1955 FACTORY WSM
TRIUMPH TWINS 1956-1969 (BOOK OF)
VELOCETTE ALL SINGLES & TWINS 1925-1970 (BOOK OF)
VESPA 1951-1961 (BOOK OF)
VESPA 125 & 150cc & GS MODELS 1955-1963 (SECOND BOOK OF)
VESPA GS & SS 1955-1968 (BOOK OF)
VINCENT MOTORCYCLES 1935-1955 WSM

www.VelocePress.com

www.ingramcontent.com/pod-product-compliance
Lightning Source LLC
Chambersburg PA
CBHW070601170426
43201CB00012B/1895